CW01509054

LENA ELLIS

The Essential Halkidiki Travel Guide

What To Know Before You Go

Copyright © 2025 by Lena Ellis

All rights reserved. No part of this publication may be reproduced, stored or transmitted in any form or by any means, electronic, mechanical, photocopying, recording, scanning, or otherwise without written permission from the publisher. It is illegal to copy this book, post it to a website, or distribute it by any other means without permission.

Printed in the United States of America

First edition

This book was professionally typeset on Reedsy.
Find out more at reedsy.com

Contents

Introduction

Welcome to Halkidiki, Greece's sun-drenched secret that locals rave about and travelers return to again and again. Shaped like a trident, this northern paradise offers three distinct peninsulas: vibrant Kassandra, wild and serene Sithonia, and the mysterious, spiritual Mount Athos.

This guide is your essential companion to exploring it all, from crystal-clear beaches and traditional villages to hiking trails, beach bars, ancient ruins, and sacred monasteries. Inside, you'll find practical tips, curated itineraries, and local insights designed to make your trip effortless and unforgettable.

So pack your sandals and sense of wonder because Halkidiki is calling, and it's about time you answered.

1

PREPARING FOR YOUR VACATION

Optimal Seasons for Visiting Halkidiki

Spring (Late March to May)

Spring in Halkidiki is one of the most underrated yet rewarding times to visit. Temperatures range between 15°C to 25°C, making it comfortable for hiking, cycling, and sightseeing. The natural scenery is at its greenest, with wildflowers blooming across the hillsides and less dust in the air compared to peak summer.

Hotels and resorts begin reopening around Easter, so while your choices may be more limited compared to July or August, the places that are open usually offer discounted rates. This period is ideal for visitors looking to avoid the high season crowd, enjoy lower prices, and still experience mild beach weather—though swimming might still be brisk in early spring, averaging 16°C to 20°C sea temperatures.

Spring is also rich in religious and cultural festivals. Greek Orthodox Easter, often in April or early May, is celebrated vibrantly across Halkidiki, particularly in villages like Arnea and Nikiti. Many bakeries and taverns prepare seasonal specialties such as tsoureki and magiritsa soup.

Outdoor activities such as wine estate tours, olive grove walks, bird-watching in wetlands like Agios Mamas, and archaeological sightseeing (Olynthos, Stageira) are particularly enjoyable in spring when the sun is not too harsh.

Summer (June to August)

This is peak season in Halkidiki. Temperatures range from 28°C to 35°C during the day and stay above 20°C at night. Sea temperatures rise to an inviting 24°C to 27°C. Beaches are in full swing, beach bars operate daily, and water sports facilities are open across both Kassandra and Sithonia.

Expect large crowds, particularly in July and August. Kassandra is the busiest, filled with both Greek and international tourists. Sithonia remains slightly more relaxed but still attracts a solid crowd in popular areas like Vourvourou and Sarti.

Accommodation rates during summer can double or even triple compared to shoulder seasons. It's strongly recommended to book rooms, ferry transfers, and car rentals months in advance. Restaurants, bars, and taverns are fully operational and often require reservations, especially in hotspots like Kalithea and Neos Marmaras.

Cultural events also reach their peak. The Sani Festival, one of Greece's premier open-air music festivals, runs through July and August and attracts world-class performers. Various village feasts (panigiria) take place, celebrating local saints and serving traditional food, music, and dancing that often continues until dawn.

For beach lovers, families, and nightlife seekers, summer is the best season to visit. However, those sensitive to heat or crowding may find the intensity overwhelming, especially during mid-August when Greeks take their own vacations.

3

Autumn (September to October)

Autumn is a shoulder season that offers the best of both worlds—summer warmth without the chaos. September still feels like summer, with daytime temperatures around 26°C and sea temperatures that remain swimmable. By mid-October, it cools down to the low 20s, and some beach taverns begin to close.

This period is especially attractive to couples, solo travelers, and digital nomads. Accommodation prices drop significantly, and beaches are less crowded. Many activities such as boat tours, snorkeling, and hiking remain available but without long waits or large group bookings.

Olive harvesting season begins in late October. Some local farms and agritourism locations allow visitors to watch or participate in the process. Wine tours are also popular, with the vintage season peaking around this time. Local festivals celebrating harvests or saints continue in more rural areas.

If you enjoy tranquil beaches, warm days, and cultural immersion without battling for space at dinner, early autumn is a prime time to go. However, by late October, some businesses begin to close for the season, particularly in smaller villages.

Winter (November to Early March)

Winter is considered off-season in Halkidiki. Many resorts, beach bars, and tourist businesses shut down. The weather is generally mild for Europe, with temperatures between 5°C and 15°C, but this is not beach weather. Rain is more frequent, especially in December and January.

However, this period can still be rewarding for travelers looking to explore the cultural and natural side of the region. Mount Athos, the monastic republic, remains open to male pilgrims all year. Traditional inland villages like Arnea and Polygyros hold winter festivities and are known for local cuisine and crafts.

Accommodation is limited but available, mostly in year-round guesthouses or city hotels in larger towns like Nea Moudania and Polygyros. Flights into Thessaloniki remain consistent throughout the year, so access is never an issue.

Winter is ideal for spiritual travelers, foodies, or those using Halkidiki as a base to explore Thessaloniki or northern mainland Greece without tourist traffic. It is not recommended for those expecting beach life or resort amenities.

Summary of Best Times by Travel Goal

- Best for Beaches and Nightlife: Mid-June to early September
- Best for Outdoor Activities and Sightseeing: Late April to early June, September
- Best for Budget Travelers: Late September to early November
- Best for Cultural Festivals and Local Life: April (Easter), August (Panigiria), October (Harvest festivals)
- Best for Tranquility and Relaxation: May, early October
- Best for Spiritual Travel: Year-round (Mount Athos access permitting)

Need to Know for Your Vacation

Currency and Payments

Greece uses the euro (€), and Halkidiki is no exception. Cash is still king, especially in rural villages, beach bars, smaller tavernas, and local markets. While credit and debit cards are widely accepted in hotels, restaurants, and chain stores, smaller businesses may not have card readers or might offer discounts for cash payments.

ATMs are common in larger towns such as Nea Moudania, Polygyros, and along the tourist strips of Kassandra and Sithonia. However, they can be sparse in more remote beach villages. It's wise to carry at least €100–€150 in cash when exploring for the day, especially if you're heading to isolated areas.

Notify your bank before travel, and be aware that foreign cards may come with transaction fees. Most ATMs charge a local withdrawal fee of €2–€4.

Language

Essential Words and Phrases

These are your must-knows—the everyday Greek words you'll actually use:

- Hello – Γειά σου (YAH-soo)
- Good morning – Καλημέρα (kah-lee-MEH-rah)
- Good evening – Καλησπέρα (kah-lee-SPEH-rah)
- Good night – Καληνύχτα (kah-lee-NEEKH-tah)
- Goodbye – Αντίο (ah-DEE-o)
- Please – Παρακαλώ (pah-rah-kah-LOH)
- Thank you – Ευχαριστώ (eff-khah-rees-TOH)
- Yes – Ναι (neh)
- No – Όχι (OH-khee)
- Excuse me / Sorry – Συγγνώμη (seen-GNO-mee)
- Do you speak English? – Μιλάτε Αγγλικά; (mee-LAH-teh ang-lee-KAH?)

Pro tip: a smile and "Yah-soo" can soften any situation. It's casual, polite, and works just about anywhere.

At a Restaurant or Café

These phrases will help you navigate menus, place orders, and avoid accidentally ordering an entire octopus (unless that's your thing):

- I would like... – Θα ήθελα... (tha EE-theh-lah...)
- The bill, please. – Τον λογαριασμό, παρακαλώ. (ton loh-ghar-yaz-MOH, pah-rah-kah-LOH)
- Water – Νερό (neh-ROH)
- Coffee – Καφές (kah-FES)
- Wine – Κρασί (krah-SEE)
- Beer – Μπύρα (BEE-rah)
- Delicious! – Νόστιμο! (NOS-tee-mo)

Menus are often in both Greek and English, especially in tourist-heavy areas, but don't hesitate to ask for help or use Google Translate when needed.

Getting Around

Need to catch a taxi or ask where the beach is? These phrases will save you time (and possibly a few wrong turns):

- Where is...? – Πού είναι...? (poo EE-neh...?)
- How much does it cost? – Πόσο κοστίζει; (POH-soh koh-STEE-zee?)
- I'm lost. – Έχω χαθεί. (EH-hoh kha-THEE)
- Left / Right / Straight – Αριστερά / Δεξιά / Ευθεία (ah-ree-ste-RAH / thek-see-AH / ef-THEE-ah)
- Bus station – Σταθμός λεωφορείων (stath-MOS le-oh-fo-REE-on)

Most bus drivers and taxi operators know basic English, but showing your destination written in Greek can really help.

7

Numbers 1–10

Greek numbers come in handy when shopping, asking about times, or haggling over souvenirs.

1 – ένα (EH-nah)
2 – δύο (THEE-oh)
3 – τρία (TREE-ah)
4 – τέσσερα (TEH-seh-rah)
5 – πέντε (PEN-deh)
6 – έξι (EH-xee)
7 – επτά (ep-TAH)
8 – οκτώ (ok-TOH)
9 – εννιά (en-YAH)
10 – δέκα (THEH-kah)

Greek Etiquette

Greeks value warmth and politeness. Here are a few cultural notes to keep in your back pocket:

- Always say "Kalimera" (Good morning) when entering shops, bakeries, or cafés. It's polite and appreciated.
- A genuine "Efharistó" (Thank you) goes a long way.
- Shaking your head "no" and saying "Nai" (which means "yes") is a very common and very confusing tourist moment. Just remember: "Nai" = "Yes," and "Ohi" = "No."
- Don't be shy. Greeks appreciate the effort, even if your accent sounds like a pizza trying to speak.

Tipping Etiquette

Tipping is not obligatory, but it is appreciated. In restaurants, rounding up the bill or leaving 5%–10% is customary. Hotel porters typically receive €1–€2 per bag, and housekeeping €1–€2 per night. For taxi drivers, rounding up the fare is sufficient.

Electricity and Plugs

Greece uses standard European Type C and Type F plugs (230V, 50Hz). If you're coming from the UK, US, or other regions, bring an appropriate adapter and possibly a voltage converter for sensitive electronics. Power outages are rare but can happen during summer storms, especially in rural or mountainous parts of Sithonia and Athos.

Healthcare and Emergency Services

Greece has a public healthcare system supplemented by private clinics. Halkidiki's main public hospital is in Polygyros. Several private clinics operate in tourist zones like Nea Moudania, Kallithea, and Neos Marmaras. Pharmacists are knowledgeable and can offer over-the-counter solutions for minor ailments.

Emergency numbers:

- Ambulance: 166
- Police: 100
- Fire: 199
- European emergency line (works from mobiles): 112

Travel insurance is strongly recommended. EU citizens with a European Health Insurance Card (EHIC) can access basic healthcare, but private clinics often require cash payment or proof of insurance.

Water, Food Safety, and Hygiene

Tap water is safe to drink in most parts of Halkidiki, especially in hotels and towns. However, some rural areas and islands might have heavily chlorinated or mineral-heavy water, so bottled water is often preferred.

Food safety standards are high. Street food and open-air grills follow local hygiene protocols, and incidents of foodborne illness are rare. That said, avoid uncooked seafood unless you're in a trusted restaurant.

Toilets in public places may lack toilet paper, so it's wise to carry tissues or travel wipes. Never flush toilet paper; plumbing systems are narrow, and bins are provided for disposal.

Connectivity and SIM Cards

Greece has good mobile coverage, and Halkidiki is generally well-connected, though mountainous or remote areas like parts of Sithonia may have patchy service.

Major Greek mobile networks include Cosmote, Vodafone, and WIND. You can buy prepaid SIM cards at Thessaloniki Airport or in towns like Nea Moudania or Polygyros. Expect to pay around €10 for a SIM with 5–10GB of data.

Wi-Fi is common in hotels, cafes, and restaurants, although speeds vary. In some cases, you may need to ask for the password, even if the sign says "Free Wi-Fi."

Local Laws and Cultural Norms

Public intoxication is frowned upon, even in party areas like Kallithea. While topless sunbathing is generally accepted on isolated beaches, it's discouraged on family beaches and in village areas.

Drugs are strictly illegal, even cannabis. Greece has a zero-tolerance policy, and penalties are severe.

Nudity is not permitted except on designated nudist beaches, such as Kavourotrypes in Sithonia. Photography inside churches and monasteries is often prohibited or restricted. For Mount Athos, only men are allowed, and permits must be obtained in advance.

Respect local customs:

- Don't enter churches or monasteries with bare shoulders or shorts.
- Don't touch or point at religious icons.
- Be polite and keep noise levels down in village areas, especially during siesta time (usually 2–5 PM).

Opening Hours and Siesta Culture

Shops generally open around 9–10 AM, close for siesta from 2–5 PM, and reopen until 9–10 PM. During peak summer months, tourist shops stay open longer. Larger supermarkets like Masoutis or Lidl often stay open through the afternoon.

Banks usually operate from 8:00 AM to 2:00 PM, Monday to Friday. Pharmacies follow the same hours, though emergency pharmacies rotate after-hours services.

Safety and Scams

Halkidiki is a safe region with low crime rates. Petty theft is rare but possible, especially in crowded beaches or festivals. Always watch your belongings, especially on public transportation or in beach bars.

Avoid:

- Accepting "free" bracelets or flowers from street sellers
- Unofficial taxis—always confirm fare before entering
- Leaving valuables visible in rental cars, especially at remote beaches

Packing Essentials

Clothing

Halkidiki has a Mediterranean climate, with hot, dry summers and mild, wet winters. If you're visiting between May and September:

- Lightweight clothing: Think breathable cotton and linen shirts, shorts, sundresses, tank tops.
- Swimwear: Bring at least two swimsuits so you always have a dry one.
- Evening attire: Casual elegance works best. Pack a sundress, polo shirt, or a linen button-down for dining out.
- Light sweater or jacket: Evenings near the coast can get breezy, especially in May and September.
- Activewear: If you're planning to hike or bike, include moisture-wicking T-shirts, athletic shorts, and a sun hat.
- Sleepwear and underwear: Pack enough to avoid frequent washing.

If you're visiting in the cooler months (October through April), include:

- A medium-weight jacket or raincoat
- Long-sleeved shirts
- Jeans or long trousers
- Scarf and closed shoes

Footwear

- Comfortable walking shoes: Essential for cobbled streets, trails, and archaeological sites.
- Sandals or flip-flops: For the beach and casual outings.

- Water shoes: Useful if you plan on exploring rocky beaches or shallow coves.
- Dressier shoes: For upscale restaurants or night spots.

Toiletries and Personal Items

- Sunscreen (SPF 30+): Greek sun is intense, especially between 11 am and 4 pm.
- After-sun lotion or aloe gel
- Insect repellent
- Travel-sized shampoo, conditioner, body wash
- Toothbrush, toothpaste, floss
- Deodorant
- Razor, shaving cream
- Feminine hygiene products
- Hairbrush or comb
- Nail clipper and tweezers
- Contact lenses and solution (if applicable)
- Prescription medication and a copy of your prescriptions

Tech and Electronics

- Phone and charger
- Portable power bank
- Camera and charger (if not using your phone)
- Travel adapter (Greece uses Type C and F plugs, 230V)
- E-reader or tablet (optional)

Beach Gear

- Beach towel or quick-dry microfiber towel
- Snorkeling gear (optional, but many coves are perfect for it)
- Waterproof phone pouch
- Foldable beach bag or tote
- Sunglasses with UV protection
- Wide-brimmed hat or cap
- Lightweight cover-up or beach robe

Documents and Money

- Passport and copies (store one copy separately)
- Travel insurance documents
- Driver's license and International Driving Permit (if renting a car)
- Credit/debit cards and some cash (euros)
- Hotel and transport reservations (digital and print copies)
- Emergency contact list

Health and Safety Items

- Mini first aid kit (band-aids, antiseptic, pain relievers, motion sickness pills)
- Reusable water bottle
- Hand sanitizer and antibacterial wipes
- Face masks (some healthcare facilities still require them)

Extras That Make a Difference

- Small daypack or crossbody bag
- Reusable shopping bag (for groceries or beach gear)
- Lightweight travel umbrella
- Journal and pen (especially for longer trips)
- Greek phrasebook or language app

Packing smart for Halkidiki is about anticipating your activities and being ready for sun, sea, and scenic strolls. Make sure your luggage is flexible enough to handle a beach day in Kassandra, a winery tour in Sithonia, and a boat trip to Mount Athos—all in one trip.

Halkidiki Vacation Cost

Accommodation Costs: From Rustic to Regal

Halkidiki's accommodation options range from €30-per-night studios to €600-per-night luxury villas. In the low season (April to early June, and late September), budget travelers can find basic rooms in smaller towns or inland villages for as little as €25–€40 per night. Mid-range hotels near the beach—especially in places like Nikiti, Neos Marmaras, or Sarti—average around €70–€120 a night in the high season (July and August). Luxury stays in resorts such as Porto Carras or Sani Resort jump significantly to €250–€500+ per night during peak times, often requiring early booking.

Airbnb and villa rentals are especially popular for families and groups. A private apartment for four near the beach might cost €100–€180 per night in July, while high-end villas with pools in Kassandra or Sithonia could go for €350–€700 per night. Booking early (at least 3–6 months ahead) often results in better rates.

Food and Drink: Taverna Life and Beyond

Dining in Halkidiki is often one of the most enjoyable parts of the trip—and it doesn't have to break the bank. A traditional Greek taverna meal, including a main course like moussaka or grilled fish, along with a salad, bread, and house wine, will typically cost €12–€20 per person. In more tourist-heavy towns like Hanioti or Pefkochori, prices may nudge up slightly, especially for fresh seafood, which can hit €25–€35 for a plate depending on the catch.

For quick meals, gyros and souvlaki are your best budget allies— expect to pay around €3–€5 each. A coffee at a seaside café runs about €3–€4, while a large local beer will set you back €4–€6. High-end restaurants, particularly those attached to resorts, offer fine dining at around €40–€70 per person for a three-course meal with wine.

Self-catering is another option, especially if you're staying in a villa or apartment with a kitchenette. Supermarkets like Masoutis and Lidl carry local and imported goods. A week's groceries for two people might cost €50–€80, depending on your tastes and how much you cook.

Transportation: Getting Around Without the Budget Bends

Transportation in Halkidiki can be one of the trickier things to budget because public transit is limited, especially in Sithonia and Athos. If you're relying on buses, a ticket from Thessaloniki to Kassandra or Sithonia costs around €10–€15 one-way. However, buses don't run frequently and often don't reach beaches or remote villages.

Renting a car is highly recommended if you want flexibility. During summer, expect to pay €35–€60 per day for a compact car. Gasoline in Greece is among the priciest in Europe—averaging around €2 per liter—so if you're planning long drives (say, exploring both Kassandra and Sithonia), factor in around €50–€100 in fuel for a 5–7 day trip. Parking is generally free in small villages, but some beach spots may charge €3–€5 per day.

Taxis are available but expensive. A ride from Thessaloniki Airport to Sani Beach, for example, can cost €80–€100 one-way. Transfers arranged by hotels or private services offer more comfort and reliability but at similar prices.

Beach Amenities and Activities: Sun, Sea...and Umbrella Fees

Most of Halkidiki's beaches are public and free to access, but many are lined with beach bars offering sunbeds and umbrellas. These are usually free with a minimum drink order (around €5–€10), but in popular spots during peak season, you may be charged €15–€25 for a set. Some luxury beach clubs charge flat entry fees of €20 or more per person, especially on weekends.

Water activities vary by location. Kayak or SUP rentals cost around €10–€20 per hour. Snorkeling tours or boat trips to nearby coves and islands can range from €25 for a group excursion to €80+ for private options. Scuba diving courses start at around €60 for beginners. If you're headed to Mount Athos for a cruise (since only men can enter the monastic community), expect to pay around €20–€30 for a day trip from Ouranoupoli.

Sightseeing and Extras: Culture Without Cost Shock

Many of Halkidiki's attractions, like Byzantine towers, monasteries, and hilltop villages, are free or charge symbolic entry fees. The Petralona Cave, for example, costs around €10 for entry. Museums are often free or very affordable—typically under €5. The same goes for small local festivals, which are often open to the public and offer free entertainment, music, and sometimes even food tastings.

Souvenirs such as local honey, olive oil, handmade soaps, and wine are reasonably priced. Expect to pay €5–€10 for a jar of premium honey, €6–€12 for a bottle of local wine, and €2–€4 for soaps and herbs. Bargaining is not common in Greece, but friendly conversation with local artisans can sometimes lead to a discount if you're buying multiple items.

Estimated Daily Budget Ranges

- Budget traveler: €50–€80/day
- Mid-range traveler: €100–€180/day
- Luxury traveler: €250–€500+/day

These estimates include accommodation, meals, transportation, and basic activities but don't account for shopping or personal splurges.

Insightful Travel Advice

1. Don't Try to Conquer All Three Peninsulas

Halkidiki is shaped like Poseidon's trident, with three "legs": Kassandra, Sithonia, and Athos. First-timers often think they can zip between all three in a few days and "see it all." Don't. Each peninsula has a different personality. Kassandra is buzzy and beach-clubby, Sithonia is wild and nature-focused, and Athos is cloaked in mystery and male-only monasticism. Pick one or two bases max and soak in the vibe instead of road-tripping yourself into exhaustion. The roads are winding, the views are distracting, and even "short drives" take longer than you think.

2. If You're Driving, Think Manual and Curvy

Most car rentals in Halkidiki (and Greece in general) are manual. If you can't drive stick, reserve an automatic early—there are few, and they book up fast, especially in summer. Also, prepare for narrow roads, unexpected goats, and sharp curves along cliffside paths. This is not a place to be distracted by your playlist. On the upside, nearly every turn rewards you with postcard-worthy coastal views or a sleepy mountain village that looks like it hasn't changed in 50 years.

3. Beach Timing Is Everything

The best beaches in Halkidiki can still get crowded, especially in July and August. Locals head out in the early afternoon and stay till sunset. Want the beach to yourself? Aim to arrive by 9:30 AM and leave before 2 PM. Bonus: the light is softer for photos, and the sand isn't scorching. If you're into skinny dipping or solitude, you'll find some secluded coves in Sithonia—just follow dirt roads marked by nothing but optimism and the occasional goat.

4. Cash Is King

While cards are accepted in most restaurants and hotels, many small shops, tavernas, kiosks, and especially beach bars are either "cash preferred" or mysteriously "have technical issues" when it's time to swipe. ATMs exist but are spaced out in rural areas, and you may be slapped with fees by both Greek and foreign banks. Always carry some euros (small notes and coins, too) for sunbeds, snacks, tips, or when you're stuck on a beach road with a watermelon vendor who only takes cash—because that happens.

5. Learn a Few Greek Words

Even if you butcher them with flair, a few Greek words go a long way. "Kalimera" (good morning), "Efharisto" (thank you), and "Parakaló" (please/you're welcome) are enough to win smiles. Most younger locals speak at least some English, but the further from tourist centers you go, the more you'll rely on hand gestures, Google Translate, and the universal language of smiling and nodding. Greeks are famously warm, but they appreciate the effort—especially in tiny villages where tourism isn't the main industry.

6. Avoid Thessaloniki Airport Sticker Shock

Flying into Thessaloniki (SKG) is the main gateway to Halkidiki. But beware: airport transfers to the region, especially to Sithonia or Athos, can cost more than your flight. Private transfers range from €70 to €150 one-way, depending on the distance. Shared shuttles are cheaper but can involve long waits. If you're renting a car, consider picking it up in Thessaloniki city (rather than the airport) to save money and avoid aggressive pricing from airport-based rental desks. Just make sure your pickup point is easily accessible via public transport or a cheap cab.

6. The Siesta Is Sacred

Between 2 PM and 5 PM, many shops and services take a mid-day break, especially in smaller towns. If you're planning to run errands, shop, or explore inland villages, do it before or after the siesta window. Restaurants and cafés usually stay open, but retail shops, post offices, and government offices will likely be shuttered, and you'll be stuck wandering around wondering where everyone went. They went home to nap. Maybe you should too—it's hot outside.

7. Respect the Pace and the Quiet

Halkidiki operates on a slower rhythm than urban Greece. Don't expect rapid-fire service in tavernas or lightning-fast check-in procedures at family-run hotels. Things are done with a side of conversation and a sprinkle of "we'll get to it when we get to it." Relax, slow your expectations, and embrace the pace. Also, keep your voice down in monasteries and hilltop villages—these aren't theme parks. They're living, breathing communities with elderly residents, children playing, and people living their everyday lives.

8. Don't Skip the Mountains

Yes, the beaches are sublime—but Halkidiki's inland villages and mountains are criminally underrated. Places like Arnaia and Taxiarchis offer a different side of the region: stone-built houses, cool air scented with pine and herbs, traditional tavernas, and no selfie sticks in sight. You'll find handmade cheeses, honey, and wine straight from small-scale producers who still crush grapes the old-fashioned way. Perfect for day trips or an overnight stay in a guesthouse for around €40 a night.

9. Pro Tip: Always Pack Beach Shoes

Many beaches in Halkidiki are sandy, but plenty have pebbles, sea urchins, or underwater rocks that can turn a graceful beach stroll into an interpretive pain dance. Beach shoes will save your feet and let you enjoy the water anywhere—from silky shores in Kassandra to wild, rocky coves in Sithonia. They also double as hiking shoes for the many unmarked but breathtaking coastal trails that thread along cliffs and pine forests.

Halkidiki Vacation Itineraries

1. The Beach Bliss Long Weekend (3 Days – Kassandra Focused)
Perfect for couples or anyone who wants sunsets, cocktails, and soft sand.
Day 1: Arrive and Ease In

- Arrive via Thessaloniki Airport and transfer to your hotel in Hanioti or Pefkochori.
- Enjoy an early evening dip at Hanioti Beach, followed by dinner at a beachfront taverna (try grilled octopus and ouzo).
- Optional: Nightcap at a beach bar or a moonlit walk on the

promenade.

Day 2: Beach-Hopping Bonanza

- Drive north to Kalithea Beach (organized, lively, great watersports).
- Head south to Glarokavos Lagoon for a more secluded experience.
- Lunch in Paliouri village for traditional mountain tavern vibes.
- Sunset swim at Possidi Cape—less crowded and crazy beautiful.

Day 3: Spa, Shop, and Depart

- Morning visit to a local spa (Loutra Agias Paraskevis is a top pick).
- Quick souvenir shopping in Afitos village—stone houses, art galleries, and charm overload.
- Head back to Thessaloniki or onward to your next Greek adventure.

2. Nature & Solitude Week (7 Days – Sithonia Focused)

For hikers, campers, readers, and introverts with style.

Day 1–2: Base in Vourvourou

- Rent a kayak or boat to explore Diaporos Island's coves and lagoons.
- Sunset hike to Livari Beach—no crowds, no noise.
- Dine on fresh fish in a taverna with your toes in the sand.

Day 3: Hidden Beaches of Sithonia

- Drive down the east coast: check out Karidi, Kavourotrypes (yes, it's hard to pronounce, but you won't forget the views), and Armenistis.
- Bring snacks and drinks—many beaches are remote and unser-

viced.

- Evening spent stargazing from your balcony or the beach.

Day 4–5: Explore the Interior

- Base yourself in Parthenonas, a beautifully restored mountain village.
- Hike Mount Itamos for views of both coasts (bring water and sun protection).
- Visit local honey and olive oil producers. Real flavors, no tourist markup.

Day 6–7: Beach and Reflect

- Return to the coast for two slow days in Toroni or Sykia.
- Swim, read, nap, repeat.
- Optional final dinner in Neos Marmaras with a bottle of local wine and no regrets.

3. Family Fun and Kid-Friendly Comfort (5 Days – Mix of Kassandra & Sithonia)

Zero chaos, maximum bonding.
Day 1: Arrival and Settle In (Stay in Nikiti or Gerakini)

- Choose a family-friendly hotel or resort with a pool.
- Easy beach time at Nikiti's town beach with shallow waters and playgrounds.

Day 2: Pirate Ship Cruise (Yes, Really)

- Join a day cruise from Ormos Panagias—most have pirate themes, music, and swimming stops.
- Kids love it. So do secretly exhausted parents.
- Return for an early family dinner and ice cream by the sea.

Day 3: Aqua Adventures & Culture Light

- Spend the day at a beach with inflatables and watersports (like Sani or Kalogria).
- Visit the Petralona Cave (cool, educational, and underground—great for hot days).

Day 4: Nature Day

- Walk or bike the trails around Sithonia's interior pine forests.
- Picnic at Agios Nikolaos village square.
- Optional: pony ride centers are available near Polygyros for little ones.

Day 5: One Last Splash

- A few hours at the beach or pool.
- Brunch with views.
- Pack slowly and enjoy one last frappé in the sun before heading home.

4. Culture and Curiosity Seeker (4–6 Days with a Dip into Athos)
History, hidden corners, and meaningful encounters.
Day 1–2: Base in Ouranoupoli (Near Mount Athos)

- Explore Ouranoupoli's Byzantine Tower and grab a sunset drink on the harbor.
- Take a boat tour around Mount Athos. You can't land if you're not male with a permit, but the views and monk-built monasteries clinging to cliffs are unforgettable.

Day 3: Religious and Historical Exploration

- Visit the ancient site of Olynthos, north of Kassandra.
- Swing by Arnaia village to explore traditional Macedonian architecture and folklore museums.

Day 4–5: Wine and Ruins

- Tour Domaine Porto Carras or Claudia Papayianni wineries—tastings included.
- End the day with a visit to ancient Stagira (home of Aristotle).
- Optional beach dinner in Olympiada with local mussels and Aristotle quotes flying over ouzo.

6th Day: Thessaloniki City Day Trip

- Drive to Thessaloniki for Byzantine churches, the Rotunda, the White Tower, and buzzing street food.
- Return to Halkidiki or continue exploring northern Greece.

Tips for All Itineraries

- Car rental is essential for anything off the main tourist drag.
- Plan for flexibility. Halkidiki is best when you leave space for

spontaneity.

- Download offline maps. Mobile signal fades in remote areas.
- Use local tavernas over tourist traps because the food is better, and prices are friendlier.

2

NAVIGATING IN AND AROUND HALKIDIKI

Air Travel to Halkidiki

If you're flying into Halkidiki, you're technically not landing *in* Halkidiki at all. The region doesn't have its own commercial airport, but don't let that fool you, getting there by air is still the fastest and most efficient option. Your gateway to the peninsula is Thessaloniki Airport "Makedonia" (SKG), a busy international hub located about 15 kilometers southeast of Thessaloniki city center and approximately 50–120 kilometers from various points in Halkidiki.

The key thing to understand is that your journey doesn't end when the wheels touch down. Thessaloniki Airport is the air hub; Halkidiki is the prize waiting just beyond. From here, the rest of the trip is by road—and with a bit of planning, it can be seamless.

International Connections: Flying In from Abroad

Thessaloniki Airport is surprisingly well-connected for a regional airport. In the warmer months, it becomes a hotspot for charter flights and low-cost airlines catering to the beach-hungry masses heading to northern Greece. Airlines such as Ryanair, EasyJet, Jet2, Transavia, Wizz Air, Aegean Airlines, and Eurowings run direct routes from cities across Europe, including London, Manchester, Milan, Frankfurt, Amsterdam, Vienna, Warsaw, and Paris.

During the high season (May through October), there are often daily flights from many of these cities. Off-season, the options are fewer but still functional—just expect to transfer through Athens or another European city if you're flying from smaller airports or traveling in winter.

For travelers outside Europe, flying into Athens first and then taking a domestic flight to Thessaloniki is often the simplest route. Aegean Airlines and Olympic Air offer several flights per day between the two cities, with a flight time of just under an hour.

Domestic Flights from Athens

If your international flight arrives in Athens, you have a couple of good options. One is to hop on a connecting flight to Thessaloniki. The Athens-to-Thessaloniki air route is one of Greece's busiest, with flights almost every hour. If booked early, these flights can be surprisingly cheap, sometimes as low as €30–€50.

Keep in mind that this route isn't always faster than traveling by train or car, especially when you factor in airport waiting times. However, if you're lugging baggage and want to avoid a 5–6 hour road trip, it's a solid bet.

Arrival Experience at Thessaloniki Airport

Thessaloniki's airport isn't enormous, but it's modern, recently renovated, and easy to navigate. You'll find standard facilities: ATMs, car rental desks, cafés, duty-free shopping, and taxis waiting out front. Signage is clear, and most staff speak enough English to help you get oriented.

Here's where your choices start diverging. Once you land, you'll need to figure out how to get to Halkidiki itself. It's not hard, but it helps to know the lay of the land.

Option 1: Renting a Car – The Smart Move

If you're comfortable driving, renting a car is arguably the best way to get to and explore Halkidiki. The peninsulas are spread out, and public transportation—while doable—isn't nearly as convenient as having your own wheels. Roads are well-maintained, traffic is generally mild (outside peak August weekends), and the scenery is breathtaking.

Car rental companies operate right inside the airport terminal, including big names like Avis, Hertz, Sixt, and Enterprise. Prices can range from €25–€50 per day depending on the season and type of car. An economy model will do just fine unless you're planning mountain excursions.

From the airport, it takes about:

- 1 hour to reach Nea Moudania (gateway to Kassandra)
- 1.5 hours to reach Nikiti (start of Sithonia)
- 2 hours or more to reach Ouranoupoli (gateway to Mount Athos)

Pro tip: Book your car in advance, especially during summer months. GPS is helpful, but Google Maps or even a good old-fashioned road map will work fine, as signs are clearly marked in Greek and English.

Option 2: Taxi or Private Transfer – Stress-Free but Pricier

If driving isn't your thing—or you just want to start your holiday in the back seat—taxis and private transfers are available right outside the arrivals terminal. Pre-booked private transfers are a popular option, especially for families or groups traveling together.

Prices vary depending on the distance and the number of passengers. Expect to pay roughly:

- €60–€80 to reach Nea Moudania or the start of Kassandra
- €90–€120 to reach Sithonia's central areas like Nikiti or Vourvourou
- €130+ for trips all the way to Ouranoupoli

Private vans for larger groups are available and can be surprisingly affordable per person when split. Most resorts and hotels will help arrange these services if asked in advance.

Option 3: Public Bus – Budget-Friendly but Clunky

Yes, you can reach Halkidiki by public bus. No, it's not the smoothest option—especially if you've just come off a long-haul flight. There's no direct bus from Thessaloniki Airport to the Halkidiki region. Instead, you'll need to:

1. Take the local OASTH bus (line 01X or 01N) or a taxi to the KTEL Halkidiki Bus Station, located about 10 km west of the airport.
2. From there, catch a KTEL intercity bus to your destination in Kassandra, Sithonia, or eastern Halkidiki.

Bus tickets are very affordable, usually under €10 for most routes, and buses run relatively frequently during the day in summer. The downside? It's slower, not always well-synced with arrivals, and limited luggage space can be frustrating. Still, if you're traveling light and watching your budget, it's a viable option.

What About Helicopters?

This isn't a joke. If you're flush with cash or planning something fancy like a wedding, luxury honeymoon, or VIP retreat, helicopter transfers are available from Thessaloniki to certain resorts in Halkidiki. Some high-end hotels can arrange these by request. It's fast, flashy, and expensive (think €1000+ per trip), but hey, it's one way to make an entrance.

Things to Keep in Mind Before You Fly

- Book early in summer. Halkidiki has exploded in popularity, and flights fill up quickly, especially budget options.
- Avoid tight connections through Athens or another EU airport if you're changing airlines. Greek domestic flights tend to run on time, but give yourself breathing room.
- Don't forget travel insurance. Delays and cancellations, while rare, do happen especially if you're flying during shoulder seasons.
- Double-check your final destination in Halkidiki before booking transfers. The three peninsulas are more spread out than they seem on a map.

Ferry Services in Halkidiki

Halkidiki's unique geography, with its three sprawling peninsulas stretching like a trident into the Aegean Sea, makes ferry travel not just a charming option, but sometimes a smart shortcut. Although Halkidiki is mostly connected by road, ferries add an extra dimension of convenience, scenic travel, and occasional necessity if you want to maximize your time or explore off-the-beaten-path spots.

Let's unpack how ferry services work in and around Halkidiki, what routes exist, and when to consider them.

Where Ferries Come into Play

Unlike the Greek islands, Halkidiki itself is a peninsula connected to the mainland by roads, so ferries don't serve as primary transport to or from Halkidiki from Athens or Thessaloniki. Instead, ferry routes operate mostly between the Halkidiki peninsulas and nearby islands, as well as local coastal spots where roads are less direct or travel times by land are long.

There are two main ferry hubs to keep in mind:

- **Ouranoupoli:** The gateway to the sacred monastic republic of Mount Athos (restricted access, more on that later) and nearby islands
- **Nea Moudania and Thessaloniki:** Departure points for short ferry rides and boat tours along the Halkidiki coast

Ferries to Mount Athos

One of the most unique aspects of Halkidiki is Mount Athos, often called the "Holy Mountain." It's an autonomous monastic state with strict entry rules—only male visitors with special permits can enter, and even then, access is limited.

Ferries from Ouranoupoli are the main way authorized visitors reach Mount Athos, docking at the main port of Dafni or other small harbors. These ferries are typically small passenger boats or small car ferries, running daily in summer months. Trips take about 20–40 minutes depending on the specific destination.

If you have the proper permit, these ferries offer the only practical way to reach the monasteries, as there are no roads open to the general public within Mount Athos.

Important to note: if you don't have a permit or aren't male, you can still enjoy the ferry ride along the coast or to nearby islands without disembarking at Mount Athos itself.

Ferries to Nearby Islands

Although Halkidiki is a peninsula, its coastal location means there are small islands just offshore, accessible by boat or ferry. Some popular ones include:

- **Diaporos Island:** Located off the coast near Sithonia, Diaporos is known for its crystal-clear waters and sandy beaches. Daily boat trips from Ormos Panagias are common in summer, especially for day-trippers wanting a serene beach escape. These boats operate more like small passenger ferries or tour boats rather than traditional ferries.
- **Amouliani Island:** The only inhabited island in the Halkidiki gulf, Amouliani lies near Ouranoupoli and is a popular spot for day trips. Ferries run regularly from Ouranoupoli, especially during peak season, with a crossing time of about 10 minutes. Amouliani offers beaches, tavernas, and a laid-back vibe, making it a favorite for families and locals.
- **Other small islets:** Occasionally you can find boats offering cruises around smaller rocky islets, perfect for swimming, snorkeling, or just scenic cruising. These are mostly charter or tour boats.

Local Coastal Ferries and Boat Tours

For those who want to mix transport with sightseeing, local ferry services double as sightseeing tours along Halkidiki's scenic coastline. These boats usually operate from ports like Nea Moudania, Ormos Panagias, and Ouranoupoli and offer routes that hop between beaches, bays, and islands.

These tours vary in length and style:

- Short trips (1-2 hours) for sunset or snorkeling
- Half-day tours combining several beach stops
- Full-day excursions with lunch and swimming breaks

Booking is usually easy—just show up at the port during high season or book through local travel agents or your accommodation. Prices are very reasonable, typically €10–€30 depending on duration and route.

Ferry Ticketing and Seasonality

Most Halkidiki ferry services run from late spring through early fall (May to September/October), when demand peaks. Outside of this window, many services reduce frequency or pause completely, so check schedules ahead if traveling in shoulder seasons.

Tickets are typically purchased at the port or from kiosks near the docks, and some companies offer online booking, especially for Mount Athos ferries and popular island routes.

If you're traveling during peak season (July and August), it's wise to buy tickets in advance, especially for Mount Athos permits and ferries, which are limited and in high demand.

Combining Ferries with Other Transport

Since Halkidiki is well connected by road, combining ferries with bus or car travel is common. For example, you might drive or take a bus to Ouranoupoli, then hop on a ferry to Amouliani Island for a day trip.

This mix allows you to experience the region's diversity—mountains, beaches, monasteries, and islands—all in one trip.

Practical Tips for Ferry Travel in Halkidiki

- Arrive early: Small ferry ports can get busy during summer mornings and late afternoons. Arriving 30 minutes before departure is smart.

- Pack light: Especially on smaller boats, luggage space is limited. Consider a daypack or small suitcase for ferry trips.
- Weather matters: Ferry schedules can be affected by weather, particularly wind and waves. If you have tight plans, keep an eye on forecasts and allow flexibility.
- Ask locals: Many hidden ferry routes or boat tours aren't well-advertised online but are popular with locals. Don't hesitate to ask your accommodation hosts or local tour operators for recommendations.
- Bring cash: Many ferry kiosks don't accept cards, especially on smaller islands or less touristy routes.

Bus Travel Across Halkidiki

Halkidiki's sprawling layout with three distinct peninsulas—Kassandra, Sithonia, and Mount Athos—makes getting around a bit of an adventure. While many travelers rent cars for freedom and flexibility, bus travel remains an affordable and practical way to explore the region, especially if you prefer leaving the driving to someone else or want a more local vibe.

Let's dive deep into how bus travel works in Halkidiki, including routes, schedules, tips, and what to expect on the road.

Who Runs the Buses?

The primary company operating buses in Halkidiki is KTEL Halkidikis, a regional branch of Greece's broader KTEL bus network. KTEL services most of Greece's regions, providing intercity and local bus connections. Halkidiki's KTEL buses cover major towns, villages, and beach areas, linking them to Thessaloniki and each other.

Buses are generally modern, air-conditioned, and reliable, though some routes, especially to smaller villages, may use older vehicles or run less frequently.

Main Routes and Destinations

Understanding Halkidiki's layout is key here. The peninsula's main transport hubs include Thessaloniki (the nearest big city), Nea Moudania, and Polygyros (the capital of Halkidiki). From these points, buses radiate out to towns, beaches, and smaller villages.

Some important bus routes:

- **Thessaloniki to Nea Moudania:** This is a busy route connecting Halkidiki with Thessaloniki's main bus station (KTEL Makedonia). Buses run frequently throughout the day, taking about 1 hour.
- **Nea Moudania to Kassandra Peninsula:** Multiple routes serve popular resort towns like Kallithea, Hanioti, Pefkochori, and more. During summer, buses run more frequently to cater to tourists.
- **Nea Moudania to Sithonia Peninsula:** Routes cover towns like Nikiti, Neos Marmaras, and Parthenonas. Travel times vary, with some routes offering direct services and others requiring transfers.
- **Polygyros (Halkidiki capital) routes:** Connects to inland villages and links up with routes to both peninsulas.
- **Thessaloniki to Ouranoupoli:** A key route for those visiting Mount Athos or nearby beaches, with buses running a few times daily, more in summer.

Frequency and Schedules

Bus frequency varies widely based on the route and season. Expect these general patterns:

- **Summer (June to September):** Most popular routes run every 30 minutes to an hour during the day, with extended evening services especially along Kassandra and Sithonia's tourist hotspots.
- **Off-season (October to May):** Bus frequency drops significantly. Some routes may only have a handful of buses per day, and weekend service may be limited or nonexistent.

Schedules are posted at bus stations and often available online through the KTEL Halkidikis website or third-party apps, but be aware they may not always be up to date, so checking locally or asking your accommodation for current info is smart.

How to Buy Tickets

Tickets can be bought directly from the driver when you board most local KTEL buses—simple, no fuss, and cash only. For longer or intercity trips starting from Thessaloniki's main bus terminal, you can buy tickets at the station or online in advance, which is handy in peak season.

Ticket prices are very affordable, generally ranging from €2–€6 for short local trips and up to €10–€15 for longer routes (like Thessaloniki to Ouranoupoli).

What to Expect on the Bus

Greek KTEL buses are generally comfortable, with air conditioning and roomy seating. However, expect some variability:

- Crowded buses in peak season: Popular tourist routes can get full, especially mid-morning and late afternoon, so boarding early is wise.
- Stop requests: On many rural routes, buses stop on request for passengers wanting to get off at smaller villages or beaches. Just

press the stop button or notify the driver.

- Luggage: Most buses have space for suitcases underneath or in overhead racks. For beach days, bring smaller bags if possible to avoid hassle.
- English signage: While major routes have English timetables and stops, rural and smaller buses may only have Greek signs. A translation app or a map helps if you're unsure.

Bus Travel vs. Renting a Car

For many visitors, bus travel is a great budget-friendly option, but it's not without limitations:

- Pros: Cheap, eco-friendly, no parking worries, local interaction, decent coverage of major destinations.
- Cons: Less flexibility (especially for hidden beaches or late-night outings), slower travel times, limited routes off the main roads.

If you're staying mainly in towns and plan day trips to well-connected spots, buses work well. For off-the-beaten-path exploration, a car or scooter rental might be better.

Tips for Making Bus Travel Work for You

- Plan around schedules: Unlike big cities, Halkidiki's buses don't run 24/7. Check departure times for return trips to avoid getting stranded.
- Ask locals: Bus drivers and station attendants can be super helpful if you ask for advice on routes or connections.
- Use a map: Halkidiki's peninsulas have winding roads and multiple bus stops; having a map or GPS can prevent missing your stop.
- Consider combo tickets: Sometimes local tour operators bundle

bus transport with guided tours, which can be a hassle-free way to explore.

- Be patient: Greek bus travel can be delightfully unpredictable. Embrace the slower pace, enjoy the scenery, and consider unexpected stops as part of the adventure.

Bus Travel for Visiting Mount Athos

Since Mount Athos is restricted to authorized visitors, the bus route to Ouranoupoli is your best bet to get close to the monastic state. From Ouranoupoli, you'll transfer to the ferry for permitted visitors. The bus schedule to Ouranoupoli aligns with ferry departures during summer, but check times closely and book your Mount Athos permit well in advance.

Accessibility

KTEL buses generally have some accommodations for people with disabilities, but services may vary by route and vehicle age. If accessibility is a concern, inquire in advance or consider private transport options.

Train Travel in Greece and How It Connects to Halkidiki

The Greek Rail System at a Glance

Train services in Greece are operated by Hellenic Train, formerly known as TrainOSE. The network primarily connects major cities and regions in the mainland, with Thessaloniki acting as a key northern hub. From Thessaloniki, you can ride south to Athens, north toward the borders, or west into Macedonia and Epirus.

The good news? Trains from Athens to Thessaloniki are now much faster and more reliable, with some services running on upgraded electric rail lines and offering comfortable, air-conditioned carriages, power outlets, and even food services.

The less-good news? There are no direct train lines into Halkidiki. None. Nada. Zip.

But don't count rail out just yet.

The Closest Train Station to Halkidiki

The nearest major train station is in Thessaloniki, the second-largest city in Greece. Located about 60–90 minutes from central Halkidiki (depending on where you're headed), Thessaloniki Railway Station is a lifeline for those coming from other parts of Greece, especially Athens.

Here's how the connection typically works:

- Take a train from Athens to Thessaloniki (around 4–5 hours).
- From Thessaloniki, transfer to a KTEL Halkidikis bus or rent a car to reach your destination in Halkidiki.

This hybrid train-bus combo isn't exactly seamless, but it's manageable with a bit of planning.

Athens to Thessaloniki by Train

If you're starting your Greek journey in Athens and want to avoid a domestic flight, the train to Thessaloniki is a scenic, budget-friendly option.

- Duration: 4–5 hours (express trains are faster)
- Frequency: 4–6 trains daily
- Cost: Around €35–€45 depending on class and availability
- Comfort: Reserved seating, clean cabins, decent legroom, and refreshments on board.

Booking in advance online at https://tickets.hellenictrain.gr ensures availability and usually nets you a better seat.

International Train Connections to Thessaloniki

Traveling from the Balkans or Central Europe? Thessaloniki is also reachable by international trains (though not daily). Some notable connections include:

- **Sofia to Thessaloniki:** Several times weekly, around 7–8 hours.
- **Skopje (North Macedonia) to Thessaloniki:** Seasonal or limited services; check schedules.

From Thessaloniki, once again, your options to Halkidiki revert to buses, cars, or taxis.

Why Take the Train at All?

You might wonder: if I can't get to Halkidiki by train, why even consider it?

Well, here's where train travel still holds its own:

- Long-distance comfort: Trains offer a more relaxed ride than cramped budget flights or overnight buses.
- Eco-conscious choice: Trains are more sustainable than flying or driving.
- Scenic routes: Especially between Athens and Thessaloniki, the ride takes you through rolling hills, coastal vistas, and rural villages.

If you're planning a multi-stop Greece itinerary—say, Athens ➜ Thessaloniki ➜ Halkidiki—train travel can anchor your journey with comfort and style.

The Missing Link: Why No Trains in Halkidiki?

This is a frequent head-scratcher for travelers. The short answer: terrain and priorities. The Halkidiki region, with its rugged peninsulas and low population density outside the summer months, hasn't justified the massive infrastructure investment needed to extend the railway system.

In the past, there were whispers of planned extensions, especially during tourism booms, but these plans have either stalled or been shelved in favor of road upgrades.

So instead of tracks, Halkidiki runs on highways, ferries, and buses—each working like pieces of a sprawling jigsaw puzzle.

Combining Train and Bus Travel

To make this work smoothly, here's a simple step-by-step for the Athens ➔ Halkidiki route using public transport:

1. **Athens ➔ Thessaloniki by train:** Depart from Athens Railway Station (Stathmos Larissis) and arrive in Thessaloniki after 4–5 hours.
2. **Walk or taxi to KTEL Halkidiki Bus Station:** It's not the same location as the train station, so allow 15–20 minutes by taxi or about 40 minutes by bus.
3. **Take a KTEL bus to Halkidiki:** Choose your peninsula (Kassandra, Sithonia, or Mount Athos) and hop on the appropriate route.

You'll need to coordinate train and bus schedules carefully, especially outside summer. Missing your connection could mean a long wait or an overnight in Thessaloniki—though honestly, that's not a bad detour.

Tickets, Timing, and Tips

- Book train tickets online: Avoid station queues, and check for delays. The Hellenic Train website is easy to use and available in English.
- Travel light: While trains have luggage space, transferring to buses or taxis is easier with less baggage.
- Pack snacks: While some trains have food service, don't count on it, and stations don't always offer much.
- Mind the strike days: Greece has an active labor movement, and occasional strikes can affect trains. Always double-check 24 hours before departure.

What if You Fly into Thessaloniki?

For those arriving by air into Thessaloniki Airport (SKG), you don't need the train at all but it's good to know that Thessaloniki's railway station is reachable from the airport by taxi (25–30 minutes) or public bus.

If you're doing a northern Greece road trip—perhaps a loop from Thessaloniki to Meteora or Mount Olympus before hitting Halkidiki—rail still fits into your itinerary as a clean and relaxing alternative to renting a car for the whole journey.

Should You Even Consider Trains if Your Trip is 100% Halkidiki?

If your sole goal is to park yourself on a beach in Sithonia for a week, then no—don't bother with trains. Fly into Thessaloniki, then take a direct bus or arrange a private transfer. Train travel is for those who are moving across regions, exploring more of Greece, or trying to see both urban and beach life.

3

TOURIST ATTRACTIONS AND LANDMARKS

Ancient Olynthus

Once a thriving ancient city and military stronghold, Ancient Olynthus offers a glimpse into urban planning from the Classical era. Its grid layout is among the earliest known examples of Hippodamian planning (the precursor to modern city blocks). Visitors can walk through the ruins of homes with intricate mosaics, including geometric patterns and mythological scenes. A modest on-site museum adds context with pottery, tools, and excavation maps.

GPS: 40.2840° N, 23.3796° E

Petralona Cave and Anthropological Museum

Known as the "Cave of the Red Stones" due to the color of its walls, this impressive limestone cave stretches over 1.5 km. Its most famous find, the **700,000-year-old Petralona Skull**, is considered one of Europe's oldest hominid remains. The cave also contains fossilized bones of extinct animals like bears, hyenas, and lions. The museum—when open—features archaeological and anthropological discoveries from the site and other parts of Greece.
  GPS: 40.3347° N, 23.0852° E

Aristotle's Park in Stageira

This outdoor educational park celebrates Aristotle's legacy with inter-active exhibits inspired by his writings on natural philosophy. Test out the "optical discs," learn about inertia and sound waves, or experience the water turbine—all with explanatory plaques. The park is set in lush greenery with panoramic views of the Gulf of Ierissos, making it both a relaxing and thought-provoking stop.
  GPS: 40.4934° N, 23.7436° E

Tower of Ouranoupoli

Standing since 1344, this tower is a rare surviving piece of Byzantine fortification in Chalkidiki. It was once a defense post for Vatopedi Monastery and later the home of Loch and Joice Sydney, a pair of philanthropists who helped preserve Mount Athos manuscripts. Today, the tower has been restored and includes photo exhibits and historical artifacts, along with access to a lovely beach.

GPS: 40.3274° N, 23.9766° E

Ammouliani Island

Ammouliani is a peaceful oasis just 15 minutes by ferry from the mainland. It combines lush greenery with serene sandy beaches such as Alikes, Megali Ammos, and Agios Georgios. The charming village features whitewashed houses and welcoming tavernas serving fresh seafood. You can also take boat tours around the nearby uninhabited Drenia islands or rent a scooter to explore the island's full coastline.
GPS: 40.3497° N, 23.9138° E

Sani Resort and Wetlands

Beyond luxury stays, the Sani area is a paradise for nature lovers. The Sani Wetlands, covering over 110 hectares, are home to rare and migratory birds like flamingos, herons, and ospreys. A network of walking and cycling trails through pine forests and lagoons is open to the public. Birdwatching kiosks, eco-tours, and nature photography make this more than just a beach destination.
GPS: 40.0953° N, 23.3122° E

Mount Athos View Cruises

While Mount Athos remains closed to women and most non-Orthodox men, these cruises are a beautiful workaround. Boats sail along the peninsula's western coastline, offering views of a dozen centuries-old monasteries—some with onion domes, others resembling fortresses.

Most cruises include historical commentary, and some offer light refreshments onboard. Departures are from Ouranoupoli, with morning and afternoon options.

Departure GPS: 40.3261° N, 23.9845° E

Nikiti Old Town

This hilltop village reveals a completely different side of Halkidiki. Its stone-built houses with wooden balconies, tiny Orthodox chapels, and bougainvillea-lined paths offer a picture-perfect Greek setting. Visit the 19th-century Church of Agios Nikitas and stop at a family-run kafeneio for Greek coffee or ouzo. The area becomes especially charming in the evening when lanterns light up the alleyways and locals gather to socialize.

GPS: 40.2197° N, 23.6614° E

4

EXPLORING THE BEST OF HALKIDIKI

Best Beaches in Kassandra

Kassandra, the westernmost peninsula of Halkidiki, is known for its electric blue waters, golden sandy stretches, and lively beach scenes. It's the go-to destination for sun-seekers looking for that perfect mix of beauty and buzz.

1. Possidi Beach

GPS Coordinates: 39.9767° N, 23.3703° E

Possidi Beach is famous for its long, narrow sandbar that stretches dramatically into the sea. It's part of the Aegeopelagitiko nature reserve, which makes it feel wild and remote, despite being relatively accessible. The contrast between the calm lagoon side and the wave-kissed outer edge makes it an interesting dual-experience beach. You can reach Possidi by car via the main Kassandra road; it's a 25-minute drive from Kallithea.

Activities to Do:

- Walk to the Possidi Lighthouse and take in panoramic views.

- Sunbathe in peace—there are few beach bars, so it's tranquil.
- Great for photography, especially during sunset.

2. Glarokavos Beach

GPS Coordinates: 39.9878° N, 23.6164° E

Located near Pefkochori, Glarokavos features turquoise waters and a partly artificial lagoon. The beach is partially organized with some beach bars and loungers, but the further out you walk, the more secluded it becomes. Reachable by car from Pefkochori in under 10 minutes.

Activities to Do:

- Snorkeling around the breakwater.
- Lounge at nearby beach bars like Navagos.
- Enjoy water sports rentals on busier days.

3. Hanioti Beach

GPS Coordinates: 39.9871° N, 23.5808° E

A family favorite, Hanioti Beach combines crystal-clear waters with soft white sand and proximity to the village's restaurants, cafes, and boutiques. You can walk from the main square of Hanioti to the beach in minutes. Buses run regularly from Thessaloniki to Hanioti.

Activities to Do:

- Paddleboarding and banana boat rides.
- Swim in shallow, child-friendly waters.
- Enjoy a beachside lunch without leaving the sand.

4. Sani Beach

GPS Coordinates: 40.0956° N, 23.3075° E

This upscale beach is part of the Sani Resort, but large parts are open to the public. Known for its pristine, Blue Flag-certified waters and luxurious feel, it's surrounded by pine forests and close to walking trails like the Sani Wetlands path. It's around a 15-minute drive from Nea Fokea.

Activities to Do:

- Kayaking or sailing excursions arranged by the resort.
- Sunset drinks at Sani Dunes or Sani Beach Club.
- Explore the nearby Sani Marina with its upscale shopping.

5. Kallithea Beach

GPS Coordinates: 40.0816° N, 23.4568° E

This beach is for those who want a mix of beach relaxation and nightlife. During the day, Kallithea Beach buzzes with activity—beach bars, volleyball courts, and energetic crowds. At night, the beachside clubs come alive. It's within walking distance of Kallithea's center.

Activities to Do:

- Jet ski rentals and parasailing.
- Partying at beach clubs like Ahoy or Angels.
- Day-to-night beach lounging and nightlife transition.

Important Details:

- Most beaches in Kassandra have both free areas and organized parts with sunbeds and umbrellas for rent.

- Parking can be a challenge in August, so arriving early is advised.
- Wear water shoes for areas with pebbles or rocky entry points like parts of Glarokavos.

How to Get There:

From Thessaloniki, Kassandra is a 1.5-hour drive. Public buses (KTEL Halkidiki) run frequently to major villages like Kallithea, Hanioti, and Pefkochori, from where local taxis or hotel shuttles can get you to nearby beaches. Renting a car is highly recommended if you plan to explore multiple beaches.

Best Beaches in Sithonia

Sithonia, the middle finger of Halkidiki's trident-shaped coastline, is a paradise of unspoiled landscapes, emerald bays, and calm waters that look like they've been Photoshopped. Less commercialized than Kassandra, Sithonia is where you go to ditch the crowds and find raw beauty.

1. Kavourotrypes Beach (aka Orange Beach)

GPS Coordinates: 40.1013° N, 23.9826° E

This hidden gem, near Sarti, is a cluster of small coves and rock formations wrapped around turquoise waters. The mix of smooth white rocks and soft sand gives it a surreal, otherworldly look. It's accessible via a dirt road and short hike—about 15 minutes off the main road from Sarti.

Activities to Do:

- Cliff-jumping from low rocks into deep water.

- Snorkeling along rock ledges.
- Climbing for views and sunbathing on smooth rock terraces.

2. Karidi Beach

GPS Coordinates: 40.1886° N, 23.8297° E

Located in Vourvourou, Karidi is arguably Sithonia's poster beach. With its shallow turquoise waters, soft white sand, and large pine trees leaning into the shore, it's postcard perfection. Parking is nearby, though limited in high season.

Activities to Do:

- Ideal for families and non-swimmers due to shallow entry.
- Pack a picnic and enjoy a shaded meal under the trees.
- Float for hours in the calm, bath-like waters.

3. Kalamitsi Beach

GPS Coordinates: 39.9857° N, 23.9907° E

This beach sits in a protected bay at the southern tip of Sithonia. It's organized with beach bars and restaurants, yet still feels chill and laid-back. You can drive right up to it, with easy access from the main coastal road.

Activities to Do:

- Rent pedal boats or kayaks.
- Enjoy seafood at beachside tavernas.
- Swim or sunbathe in the calm cove.

4. Tigania Beach

GPS Coordinates: 40.0024° N, 23.9755° E

A secluded, Instagram-famous spot that feels like the Caribbean with Greek subtitles. It features a quirky beach bar, artistic décor, and a winding dirt road to get there. Just north of Kalamitsi, you'll need a confident driver or a local guide.

Activities to Do:

- Chill at the eccentric beach bar.
- Lounge on Balinese-style daybeds.
- Snorkel around the rocks in solitude.

5. Trani Ammouda (Ormos Panagias Beach)

GPS Coordinates: 40.2484° N, 23.7351° E

A long, wide beach with powdery white sand and vivid blue waters. It's great for both relaxing and active beach days. There are fewer crowds here than at Karidi, even in August. Easy to reach by car; just follow signs from Ormos Panagias.

Activities to Do:

- Perfect for long beach walks.
- Great for swimming and beach volleyball.
- Launch point for Mount Athos boat cruises.

Important Details:

- Sithonia's beaches are often semi-organized or completely wild, so bring shade and snacks.
- Dirt roads are common—renting a compact SUV or at least a car with decent clearance is smart.

• Many beaches lack lifeguards; swim with awareness.

How to Get There:

From Thessaloniki, Sithonia is about a 2-hour drive. There are limited buses to major villages like Nikiti, Sarti, and Neos Marmaras, but for beach-hopping, a rental car is basically mandatory. For Karidi or Trani Ammouda, the route through Nikiti is fastest.

Secluded & Hidden Coves

Kriaritsi Beach and Surrounding Coves
GPS Coordinates: 39.9867° N, 23.9744° E

Kriaritsi is not just a beach—it's a labyrinth of coves. Located in the southeastern corner of Sithonia, it features multiple isolated mini-bays, some accessible by foot, others only by sea. The beach itself is partially organized, but wander a few minutes in either direction and you'll find narrow trails that lead to untouched coves framed by white rocks and wild flora. Each one feels like your own private Aegean sanctuary. The sand is soft, the water is clear and warm, and it's common to have an entire cove to yourself—even in peak season. Some are clothing-optional by default, thanks to the privacy.

Porto Paradiso (Secret Bay near Armenistis)
GPS Coordinates: 40.1896° N, 23.9715° E

This hidden gem is near the larger Armenistis campsite beach, but most people never see it. A narrow walking path winds down to a tiny bay with shallow turquoise water and soft white sand, completely surrounded by rocks and pine trees. The quiet here is only broken by cicadas and the occasional splash of a fish. It's perfect for reading, meditating, sketching, or just escaping the digital chaos of life. Getting there means hiking down a trail, so wear decent footwear and pack light. But once you're on the sand, you'll feel like you've stepped into a Greek dreamscape no guidebook knows about.

Linaraki Small Bay (Near Sykia)

GPS Coordinates: 39.9812° N, 23.9720° E

Near the more developed Linaraki Beach and its adjacent tavernas lies a series of tiny, rocky coves that few people explore. These aren't beaches in the traditional sense—more like sea-level cradles made by the rocks—but they offer a unique experience. The water here is deeper, and the seabed is rocky and colorful, making it an unexpected hotspot for snorkeling. The cliffs offer natural sunbathing platforms and incredible views of Mount Athos in the distance. It's romantic, raw, and best visited in the early morning or late afternoon when the light turns golden and the sea becomes like glass.

Activities to Do There

Swimming in these coves is pure magic. The waters are usually calm and clear, and since most of these spots are rocky rather than sandy, they're ideal for those who enjoy long, reflective floats or leisurely dips without battling waves or kids with inflatable flamingos.

Snorkeling is another highlight. These hidden spots often have underwater rock gardens teeming with sea life. The lack of crowds means fish aren't shy, and you can often spot starfish, sea urchins, and the occasional octopus tucked under a stone ledge.

You can also explore by kayak or SUP. Renting a kayak from a nearby village like Sarti or Vourvourou and paddling to a quiet bay is the kind of adventure that makes a vacation unforgettable. You'll glide past caves, reefs, and untouched coastline, discovering spots that even locals haven't named.

For the creatively inclined, these quiet spaces are perfect for painting, photography, or journaling. The light and shadow play on the rocks and water, especially around golden hour, is unreal.

Important Details

- Most of these coves are not accessible by public transport. You'll need a rental car or scooter, and occasionally a short hike to reach them.
- Bring everything you need: water, snacks, sun protection, snorkeling gear, and maybe a trash bag to leave no trace. There's usually no shade or services.
- Many of the paths to these coves are not marked on Google Maps. Use GPS coordinates, satellite view, and offline maps.
- Flip-flops won't cut it on the rocky trails. Wear solid sandals or walking shoes.
- Cell service may be weak or nonexistent. Download offline maps or tell someone where you're going in advance.

How to Get There

From Thessaloniki, head southeast on the Egnatia Odos highway and follow signs to Sithonia. For Kriaritsi, take the road from Sykia, then follow a long, unpaved track downhill. You'll pass several camping zones and then reach the main beach—park and explore the side trails on foot to discover the secluded coves.

To reach the hidden bay near Armenistis, navigate toward Armenistis Camping. Park outside the campsite area and follow a coastal path eastward, past the main beach. Look for narrow offshoot trails toward the water. It's not officially marked but visible on satellite view.

Linaraki's small coves are best reached by driving to Linaraki Beach and walking north or south along the rocky coast until you find a private spot.

Snorkeling and Scuba Diving Spots

Kelifos Island (aka "Turtle Island")
GPS Coordinates: 40.1557° N, 23.7084° E

Located between the peninsulas of Kassandra and Sithonia, Kelifos Island is uninhabited, beautifully rugged, and only reachable by boat. Its waters are a dream for divers and snorkelers alike. The north side of the island is a hotspot for scuba diving, with steep walls, caves, and tunnels that create a playground for octopuses, groupers, moray eels, and even the occasional monk seal if you're lucky. Visibility here is usually over 30 meters on a good day.

Kavourotrypes Coves (Sithonia)
GPS Coordinates: 40.1656° N, 23.8239° E

This collection of small bays and coves between Armenistis and Sarti looks like something out of a Caribbean fantasy. Above the water, the smooth white rocks and turquoise sea are hypnotizing—but below the surface, the marine life takes over. With shallow drop-offs, large rocks that act as coral substitutes, and clear visibility, it's ideal for beginner snorkelers and free divers. Sea bream, rainbow wrasse, and anemones are common here. The natural underwater topography also makes for some great underwater photography, even with just a GoPro.

Nea Skioni Reef (Kassandra)
GPS Coordinates: 39.9393° N, 23.5376° E

Just offshore from the village of Nea Skioni lies a reef that's become a favorite among scuba instructors. It's accessible via short boat ride or even a long swim on calm days. The site features a combination of rocky bottom and patches of sea grass, where cuttlefish, nudibranchs, and the occasional stingray dwell. Because of its relatively shallow depth (10–18 meters), it's a great choice for Open Water certified divers or for final check-out dives in training.

Pirgadikia Bay (Near Ammouliani)

GPS Coordinates: 40.3502° N, 23.7545° E

While not as famous as the other areas, Pirgadikia's bay offers both shore dives and rich snorkeling opportunities. Rocky slopes extend down into the deep, with crevices hiding crabs, small lobsters, and soft corals. Since this area is less frequented, it often feels like your own private marine park. The visibility is strong and the lack of boats or water traffic makes it especially appealing for long, uninterrupted swims.

Activities to Do There

Snorkeling here isn't just about floating around—it's about slow exploration. In Kavourotrypes, you can glide from one cove to another, popping your head above water to admire the pine-covered cliffs, and then diving back under to follow curious fish around natural rock arches. Many people combine their snorkeling here with a picnic on the warm, smooth rocks.

Scuba diving at Kelifos Island is a more immersive adventure. Dive centers in Nikiti or Neos Marmaras offer boat trips with experienced instructors. If you're new, you can take an intro dive that lets you experience the magic without needing full certification. For those already certified, deeper dives reveal walls covered in coral-like flora and schools of barracuda drifting like ghosts in the blue.

In Nea Skioni, reef diving is ideal for underwater photographers. Early morning dives are particularly good for catching marine creatures in action—octopuses changing colors, crabs scavenging for breakfast, and even sea horses near the grasses if you're lucky and observant.

If you're not into diving deep, many of these locations are excellent for freediving or simply practicing breath-hold techniques in safe, shallow waters. And for families or first-timers, snorkeling excursions with local guides provide equipment, safety tips, and marine biology fun facts that turn a swim into a mini nature safari.

Important Details

- You can rent snorkeling gear at most beach towns in Sithonia and Kassandra, but for better quality and fit, bring your own.
- Several certified diving centers are located in Nikiti, Neos Marmaras, and Ouranoupoli. They offer courses, guided dives, and boat tours to remote sites.
- Best visibility for diving and snorkeling is between late May and early October, especially on calm days with minimal wind.
- Always check local weather and sea conditions before going out, especially if you plan to snorkel or dive from a boat.
- Don't touch the marine life or corals, even if they seem safe. Some are protected species or extremely sensitive to human contact.
- Some of the top dive sites, especially around Kelifos and Pirgadikia, require boat access—ask your dive center about shared trips if you're traveling solo.

How to Get There

To reach Kelifos Island, you'll need to book a boat tour from Nikiti or Neos Marmaras. Most dive centers offer daily excursions that include transportation, gear rental, and instructor guidance. These trips usually last half a day and can be combined with stops at nearby beaches.

For Kavourotrypes, drive toward Sarti and look for the unmarked dirt paths leading down to the coves between Platanitsi and Armenistis. It's best to go early in the morning before it gets crowded. Park at the top and hike down with your gear.

To reach the reef near Nea Skioni, drive to the town and ask locals or your hotel about the best access point. Some private boat operators offer snorkeling tours, or you can swim out if you're a confident swimmer. Dive centers in the area can provide guided experiences.

Pirgadikia Bay can be reached by car from Ouranoupoli or from Sithonia's eastern side. The road is scenic and the bay is peaceful—there's even a small village where you can grab lunch after your underwater escapades.

Boat Tours and Sailing Adventures

Departure Hubs and Key Routes

Neos Marmaras Marina (Sithonia)

GPS Coordinates: 40.0958° N, 23.7843° E

Neos Marmaras is a major sailing and boating hub on the Sithonia peninsula. From its marina, you can join shared catamaran cruises, private yacht charters, and traditional kaiki boat tours. Many excursions head toward the islets of Spalathronisia or the secluded shores near Porto Carras. Sunset cruises are popular here, with drinks on deck and a view of the sun melting behind the pine-covered hills.

Ouranoupoli Port (Near Mount Athos)

GPS Coordinates: 40.3281° N, 23.9804° E

For those fascinated by monastic history but unable to enter Mount Athos (especially women, who are not permitted to visit), a boat tour from Ouranoupoli is the next best thing. Boats cruise the coast of the peninsula, keeping a respectful 500-meter distance, and provide excellent views of the ancient monasteries clinging to the cliffs—some over 1,000 years old. You'll hear stories about the monastic republic and may even spot monks walking along remote paths.

Ormos Panagias (Sithonia)

GPS Coordinates: 40.2503° N, 23.7389° E

A small fishing village that now doubles as a key departure point for day cruises, Ormos Panagias offers excursions to Ammouliani Island, Mount Athos, and snorkeling adventures around Diaporos Island. The Diaporos area, in particular, is beloved for its shallow, transparent waters and uninhabited islets.

Paliouri Marina (Kassandra)

GPS Coordinates: 39.9389° N, 23.6854° E

Located at the southern tip of Kassandra, this lesser-known marina is the launchpad for boat tours to the Toroneos Gulf. You'll cruise along unspoiled shores, jump off the boat into turquoise waters, and sometimes stop at fish taverns reachable only by sea. It's ideal for those wanting a quieter experience with fewer tourists.

Activities to Do There

A typical day on the water starts with boarding a boat around 10:00 AM. Depending on the route, the first stop might be a hidden cove or a shallow bay for swimming. Around Diaporos Island, you'll find what locals call the "Blue Lagoon"—a narrow channel between islands where the water is so vividly turquoise it feels Photoshopped in real life. Snorkeling here is encouraged, and most tours provide the gear.

If you're on a cruise around Mount Athos, the focus shifts from diving in to gazing out. Each monastery is introduced via onboard narration (sometimes in multiple languages), giving you insight into the traditions and architecture of this sacred place. Binoculars are usually passed around so you can get a better look at the fresco-covered walls, hanging balconies, and small harbors where monks come ashore.

Some sailing trips include stops at remote beaches only accessible by sea. There, you can lounge in solitude, take a nap under the boat's awning, or share grilled fish and ouzo prepared onboard. In some cases, the captain might even let you help steer or hoist the sails if you're feeling adventurous.

In the evening, sunset cruises create a romantic, peaceful vibe. The sun sets slowly behind Sithonia's rugged silhouette while you drift on still waters with soft music playing and maybe a glass of wine in hand. It's not unusual for dolphins to make an appearance—especially in the Toroneos Gulf, where they often swim alongside boats.

For families, pirate-themed cruises and glass-bottom boats are also available in places like Pefkochori and Nikiti, adding a whimsical twist to the sea adventure.

Important Details

- Most boat tours operate from May to early October. July and August are the busiest—book in advance.
- Some tours include meals, drinks, and snorkeling equipment, but always double-check before booking.
- Bring sunscreen, a hat, a towel, and a light jacket for evening trips— sea breezes can be chilly after sundown.
- Wear swimwear under your clothes as many boats have no changing rooms.
- For Mount Athos tours, binoculars and a camera with good zoom are highly recommended.
- Most sailing adventures range from €35 to €90 per person, depending on the length and inclusions. Private charters can cost

more.

How to Get There

To catch a boat from Neos Marmaras, drive or bus south from Nikiti along the Sithonia coastal road. The marina is well-marked and has parking available, though it fills up quickly during peak season.

For Ouranoupoli, drive east through the Athos peninsula or take a bus from Thessaloniki. The town is the main access point for Mount Athos pilgrimages, so it's well-connected and tourist-friendly. The port is central and easy to find.

Ormos Panagias is best accessed by driving from Vourvourou or Nikiti. The village has a small central square and harbor area where boats line up for departure.

Paliouri Marina is at the very end of the Kassandra peninsula. You'll need to drive down through Pefkochori and follow signs to the marina, where parking is often free near the dock.

Day Trips to Ammouliani Island

Ammouliani is a tiny island that punches far above its weight in charm, serenity, and sea views. Tucked between the Sithonia and Athos peninsulas, it's the only inhabited island in Central Macedonia and a favorite for locals looking to unplug. With its fine-sand beaches, crystal-clear waters, and relaxed, slow-paced vibe, Ammouliani makes for a perfect day trip from mainland Halkidiki—accessible, beautiful, and somehow still under the radar of mass tourism.

Where It Is and How to Get There

GPS Coordinates: 40.3466° N, 23.9372° E

To reach Ammouliani, you'll need to first get to the port of Trypiti, located just a few kilometers west of Ouranoupoli at the northeastern tip of Halkidiki. The drive from Thessaloniki to Trypiti takes about 2.5 hours, heading east through Polygyros and then south toward Ouranoupoli. There's ample parking near the port, and ferries to the island run frequently throughout the day, especially in summer. The ferry ride takes only 15 minutes and offers beautiful views of the Aegean and the mountainous silhouettes of Athos in the distance.

Once you land on Ammouliani, you can either explore the island on foot, rent a bike, or hire a buggy. For a full day trip, renting a small scooter or ATV is the best way to make the most of your time and explore multiple beaches at your own pace.

Activities to Do There

Your day can begin in Ammouliani village itself, the island's small and only real town. It's a picturesque cluster of whitewashed houses, narrow lanes, and waterfront tavernas. You might stop for a morning coffee and a traditional "bougatsa" pastry before heading off to the beaches. The harborfront is also lined with small souvenir shops and cafes shaded by tamarisk trees.

Next, head straight to Alykes Beach, located on the southwest side of the island. This is arguably Ammouliani's most famous beach, known for its velvety sand and Caribbean-like waters. The bay is well protected from the wind, making it ideal for a long, lazy swim. It has a few organized loungers and beach bars, but there's still plenty of space to spread out your towel and enjoy some quiet. The water here is warm, shallow, and ideal for kids or casual snorkeling.

From Alykes, you can venture further to Karagatsia Beach, a more secluded spot with dramatic cliffs and emerald green water. It's accessible by a dirt road, so it's a bit trickier to reach but very worth the effort. Karagatsia is great for a peaceful swim and has less foot traffic, especially in the early afternoon. You may even see locals fishing from the rocks nearby.

In the mood for some boat action? Many visitors choose to rent a small motorboat from the main port—no license required. This allows you to circle around Ammouliani and visit nearby Drenia Islands (also called Donkey Islands). These are tiny uninhabited islets just south of Ammouliani, boasting shallow turquoise waters, white sandbanks, and a Robinson Crusoe feel. Anchor off one of these islets, jump in the water, snorkel along the rocks, or just lie back on the deck and enjoy the sun.

For lunch, head back to the main village and eat at a waterfront taverna. Many offer freshly caught seafood—grilled octopus, fried calamari, and mussels saganaki are house favorites. Pair your meal with a glass of chilled ouzo or tsipouro, and don't be surprised if the owner comes out to chat. Ammouliani is small enough that hospitality feels personal.

In the afternoon, if you're not quite ready to return to the mainland, make one last stop at Megali Ammos Beach, at the southeastern end of the island. It's a quiet strip of coast ideal for unwinding. By late afternoon, most day-trippers are either back on the ferry or at the tavernas, so you might have the beach to yourself.

You can wrap up the day back at the port, where you'll board your return ferry just in time to watch the sunset from the upper deck.

Important Details

- The Trypiti ferry to Ammouliani runs approximately every 30 minutes during the high season and costs around €2–€3 per person one way. Vehicles can also be ferried over for an additional fee.
- Boat rentals (no license required) average around €60–€90 for a

half-day, including fuel. Book in advance in July and August.

- Most beaches are reachable via rough, unpaved roads. Wear comfortable shoes or rent a suitable vehicle (buggy or ATV).
- Limited gas stations and ATMs—fill up and carry some cash just in case.
- Even on the island, accommodation is available if you decide to extend your stay, but for day-trippers, make sure to check the last ferry time.

Mount Athos Experience

Mount Athos is more than a mountain—it's a living spiritual monument, a place frozen in time where monastic life has remained largely unchanged for over a thousand years. Also known as the "Holy Mountain," it forms the easternmost peninsula of Halkidiki and operates as an autonomous monastic state under Greek sovereignty. Home to 20 Eastern Orthodox monasteries, Mount Athos is one of the most unique destinations in Europe—but there's a catch. Only men are allowed to set foot on it, and even then, a special permit is required. But that doesn't mean everyone else has to miss out. There are multiple ways to experience its majesty, even without stepping ashore.

Where It Is and How to Get There

GPS Coordinates: 40.1528° N, 24.3302° E

Mount Athos occupies the entire eastern leg of Halkidiki and is most visible from the town of Ouranoupoli, located at the edge of the restricted zone. Ouranoupoli is the last point civilians can travel to by land and acts as the launchpad for both pilgrimage and sightseeing journeys.

If you're planning to admire Mount Athos from the outside, the easiest way is by boat. Regular cruises depart from the ports of Ouranoupoli and Ormos Panagias (on the Sithonia peninsula). From Thessaloniki, it's about a 2.5-hour drive to Ouranoupoli or Ormos Panagias. Both offer ample parking and cruise ticket booths on the promenade.

Activities to Do There

Start your day early in Ouranoupoli, grabbing breakfast at a café overlooking the sea. The town itself is charming, with small shops selling religious icons, handmade soaps, and local olive products. But the real draw is the experience waiting just offshore.

Your first activity should be a Mount Athos boat cruise—this is the most accessible and visually spectacular way to witness the Holy Mountain. These cruises last around 3–4 hours and sail along the western coast of the peninsula, offering views of several of the monasteries. The boats maintain a legal distance of 500 meters from the shore (in accordance with Athonite regulations), but even from that distance, the views are nothing short of magical. You'll see cliff-perched monasteries like Dionysiou, Gregoriou, and Simonopetra, with their gravity-defying construction and Byzantine architecture rising from the rugged landscape.

As the boat glides along the coast, you'll hear a guided narration (usually in multiple languages) detailing the history of each monastery, monastic customs, and Mount Athos's role in Orthodox Christianity. The cruise also offers stunning views of Mount Athos itself—a 2,033-meter peak often wrapped in a halo of mist or clouds, lending the entire experience a mystical air.

If you're lucky, you might catch a glimpse of the monks going about their daily rituals, gardening, fishing, or walking in black robes with heads bowed. Some cruises even have binoculars on board so you can see more detail from a distance.

Back on land, you can deepen your understanding of Mount Athos by visiting the Christian Exhibition Center of Ouranoupoli, where you'll find a collection of icons, manuscripts, and photos that provide further insight into Athonite life. If you're hungry afterward, Ouranoupoli has several excellent tavernas that serve monk-inspired dishes like lentil stew, wild greens with olive oil, and hearty fish soups.

For women and anyone who cannot enter Mount Athos, the spiritual experience is still accessible in an emotional and intellectual sense. The peace of the boat tour, the reverence with which locals speak of the mountain, and the sheer physical beauty of the land itself can be deeply moving.

Now, if you're a male traveler and would like to actually enter Mount Athos, the process requires some advance planning. First, you'll need to apply for a special entry permit called a *diamonitirion*, which is granted to only a limited number of non-Orthodox visitors per day. Applications must be made several weeks in advance through the Pilgrims' Bureau of Mount Athos in Thessaloniki. Once approved, you can take a boat from Ouranoupoli to the port of Dafni and from there travel by bus or boat to various monasteries.

Inside Mount Athos, you'll stay in the monasteries as a guest, free of charge, though donations are appreciated. The experience is unlike anything else: monks chanting ancient hymns in candlelit chapels, communal meals in silence, and hours spent in contemplation surrounded by wild, untouched nature.

Important Details

- Women are not allowed to enter Mount Athos under any circumstances (a tradition dating back over 1,000 years).
- Men who wish to visit must apply for a permit at least one month

in advance via the Pilgrims' Bureau in Thessaloniki.

- Daily visitor numbers are strictly limited: 100 Orthodox and 10 non-Orthodox men per day.
- Cruises around Mount Athos (no disembarkation) are available to everyone and typically cost €25–€35 per person.
- Bring binoculars for a closer view of the monasteries during the cruise.
- Modest clothing is encouraged out of respect, even on the cruise.

Olive Oil and Wine Estate Tours in Halkidiki

Beyond the turquoise coastline, Halkidiki nurtures something just as golden—its olive oil and wine traditions. These aren't factory-style tours. They're sensory deep-dives into age-old practices, scenic landscapes, and flavors that express the soul of the land. Whether you're strolling through sunlit groves or sipping wine with a sea breeze at your back, this is slow travel at its finest.

Domaine Porto Carras – The Crown Jewel of Sithonia

Stretching across the sun-drenched slopes of Mount Meliton near Neos Marmaras, Domaine Porto Carras is a titan among Greek vineyards. Once the darling of European royalty and intellectuals, it remains one of the largest organic vineyards in Europe, blending innovation with ancient wine-making roots.

Visitors are taken on a journey through lush rows of Limnio, Malagouzia, and Assyrtiko vines. You'll witness sustainable farming practices firsthand before heading into cool cellars lined with French oak barrels. Wine tastings are typically served with local cheeses, olives, and freshly baked bread, highlighting the region's culinary synergy.

Your guide might point out that Limnio was referenced by Aristotle—who just so happened to be born nearby. In fact, every element of your visit is rooted in the past while shaped for today's curious traveler.

Key Info for Domaine Porto Carras:

- **Location:** Near Neos Marmaras, Sithonia
- **GPS Coordinates:** 40.0514° N, 23.7792° E
- **Getting There:** About 2 hours from Thessaloniki by car via Nikiti
- **Best Time to Visit:** April to October; ideal for grape harvests in September–October
- **What Makes It Special:** Historic Limnio varietal, one of the largest organic vineyards in Europe

Gaia Oliva – A Hands-On Olive Oil Haven in Polygyros

For a more intimate encounter with local flavors, head inland to Gaia Oliva near Polygyros. Here, you're not just observing olive oil production—you're immersed in it. The estate is run by a passionate family who inherited century-old olive trees and transformed their groves into a boutique, cold-press facility.

A tour typically begins with a walk through the groves, where you'll learn the difference between native olive types and what makes Halkidiki's olives some of the most sought-after in Europe. In the processing area, you'll witness the cold-pressing technique that ensures freshness and preserves nutritional value.

Afterward, guests are invited to taste various olive oils—some infused, some raw—drizzled over farm-fresh tomatoes and warm bread. The tasting often evolves into a mini masterclass, teaching you how to identify quality oils and avoid supermarket scams. It's sensory, satisfying, and surprisingly eye-opening.

Key Info for Gaia Oliva:

- **Location:** Near Polygyros, Central Halkidiki
- **GPS Coordinates:** 40.3746° N, 23.4430° E
- **Getting There:** Around 1 hour from Thessaloniki via Nea Moudania
- **Best Time to Visit:** October to December (olive harvest and pressing season)
- **What Makes It Special:** Family-run, cold-pressed oil, interactive tasting experience

Multi-Estate Tastings and Hidden Treasures

If you want to broaden your flavor palette, consider joining a guided olive and wine route through lesser-known spots like Arnea or Metagitsi. These villages offer a rustic charm and welcome you into boutique wineries and ancient olive farms where the owners might hand you a glass and start telling family stories before you've even stepped out of the car.

Vineyards in Arnea often produce bold reds with a unique mineral touch, thanks to the mountainous soil. In Metagitsi, olive farmers pride themselves on preserving heirloom trees and hand-harvesting techniques. Some estates even blend local mythology into the experience, adding a layer of folklore to every taste.

Olive oil and wine in Halkidiki aren't just ingredients, they're expressions of place. They're sipped and drizzled with the same reverence as a good story or a family tradition. When you walk these groves or toast under a fig tree, you connect to a way of life that values patience, soil, and soul.

Forest Walks and Nature Hikes

1. Mount Itamos, Sithonia

Where it is: Near Nikiti, Sithonia peninsula
What to do: Hike the Itamos Trail

Mount Itamos is the highest point in Sithonia and the perfect spot for a moderate hike with epic views. The trail begins just outside the village of Nikiti and takes you through thick pine forests, wild herbs, and rocky paths. The full trail is about 12 km (round trip) and takes 3–4 hours to complete.

At the summit, you'll find an old fire lookout post with panoramic views of the Aegean Sea, Kassandra peninsula, and even Mount Athos on a clear day. Along the way, keep your eyes peeled for wild goats, hawks, and possibly a slow-moving tortoise.

Activities:

- Hiking and photography
- Birdwatching
- Wild herb spotting (especially thyme, oregano, and mint)

2. Dragoudeli Forest, Sithonia

Where it is: Inland Sithonia, near the villages of Sykia and Parthenonas
What to do: Follow off-the-beaten-path trails

This thick, mysterious forest is less developed and ideal for more adventurous walkers. Dirt paths and shepherd trails crisscross the area, offering solitude and a true back-to-nature experience. Because signage is limited, it's best to use GPS or go with a local guide.

There's a rewarding circular hike starting from Sykia that takes you through dense forest and past scenic ridges, with glimpses of both the Strymonian and Toroneos gulfs. Autumn here is especially beautiful, with golden leaves and mushrooms everywhere.

Activities:

- Backcountry hiking
- Nature photography
- Foraging in the fall (mushrooms, chestnuts)

3. Livari Lagoon & Karidi Forest Trail, Vourvourou

Where it is: Near Vourvourou, Sithonia

What to do: Combine a forest walk with a lagoon and beach visit

For a family-friendly and low-intensity nature experience, this area is perfect. The Livari Lagoon is a calm, mirror-like body of water that you can walk around, followed by a short forest trail that leads to the famous Karidi Beach. It's flat, easy to follow, and incredibly scenic.

You'll walk through pine forest that hugs the coastline, past sand dunes and coves. It's ideal for a morning stroll or sunset walk, with the reward of a swim waiting at the end.

Activities:

- Easy walking
- Swimming and snorkeling at Karidi Beach
- Wildlife watching (look for flamingos and herons in the lagoon)

4. Holomontas Mountains, Central Halkidiki

Where it is: Around Arnea, Taxiarchis, and Varvara villages

What to do: Explore highland trails in a cooler climate

Central Halkidiki trades the sea for the mountains—and the Holomontas range is its wild green heart. The forests here are filled with oak, beech, and fir trees, and offer a different hiking experience—

cooler temperatures, dense canopy, and a totally different vibe from the coastal trails.

One of the most popular hikes is the **Varvara Waterfalls trail**, which leads you to two lush waterfalls deep in the forest. Start from the village of Varvara and follow signs toward the falls—it's a moderate 2–3 km walk, but feels like a fairytale scene, especially in spring.

Near the village of Taxiarchis, there are also multiple trails through fir forests, some of which connect to panoramic viewpoints or picnic areas. You can even visit during winter if you're into frost-covered forests and winter hiking.

Activities:

- Hiking to waterfalls
- Forest bathing and picnicking
- Visiting local mountain villages before/after your hike

5. Kassandra Pine Forest Trail, Kallithea to Kryopigi

Where it is: On the Kassandra peninsula, between two popular villages

What to do: Easy hike or walk with sea views

Though Kassandra is more touristy, it still has a peaceful pine forest between Kallithea and Kryopigi. The trail is about 4 km and runs parallel to the coastline, offering sea glimpses through the trees. It's flat and manageable, great for a morning walk before the beach.

Because the path follows the natural slope toward the sea, there are little offshoots you can follow down to secluded beach spots if you're up for a dip. It's especially popular among joggers and locals out for a daily walk.

Activities:

- Easy walking or running

- Quick beach detours
- Perfect for families and casual walkers

Guided Nature Tours

If you'd rather not go solo, several eco-tourism outfits in Halkidiki offer guided hiking tours. These often include transport, snacks, and info on local flora, fauna, and mythology. Some guides even lead moonlight hikes, where the forest becomes a completely different world.

Tips Before You Go:

- Wear sturdy hiking shoes, even for short trails
- Bring water, natural springs aren't always reliable
- Check weather, especially for mountain routes
- Avoid hiking in the hottest hours (12–4 p.m.) in summer
- Use apps like Komoot or AllTrails for GPS-guided routes
- Respect nature: don't litter, and never light fires

Traditional Villages and Hilltop Escapes

Arnea: A Tapestry of Stone, Color, and Craft
GPS Coordinates: 40.4366° N, 23.5994° E
How to Get There: From Thessaloniki, it's about a 1.5-hour drive (95 km). Take the EO Thessalonikis–Ierissou road east through Polygyros, then follow signs toward Arnea via Megali Panagia.

Arnea is nestled in the Holomontas mountain range and feels like a living museum of Macedonian architecture. Stone houses with brightly painted shutters line narrow streets, and traditional balconies overflow with flowers in spring and summer. The Historical and Folklore Museum offers a glimpse into the area's traditions, and the Church of Agios Stefanos features a glass floor revealing ruins below. You can enjoy honey tasting, sip tsipouro under the plane tree in the main square, or go for a short forest walk in autumn when the foliage blazes with color.

Parthenonas: The Comeback Village

GPS Coordinates: 40.1004° N, 23.7662° E

How to Get There: From Neos Marmaras, take the winding uphill road toward Parthenonas (about 6 km, 15 minutes by car). A taxi or rental car is ideal due to the limited public transport.

Once nearly abandoned, this village has come back to life through loving restoration. Built on the slopes of Mount Itamos, it offers breathtaking views of the Toroneos Gulf. The tiny Folklore Museum and charming stone houses create a tranquil atmosphere. You'll find quaint tavernas perfect for lunch, hiking trails starting right at the village edge, and, if you're lucky, low-key art events or traditional music nights hosted by the locals.

Taxiarchis: Fir Trees and Local Flavor

GPS Coordinates: 40.4457° N, 23.4670° E

How to Get There: Located about 75 km from Thessaloniki. Follow the road to Polygyros and continue northwest toward the Holomontas forest area. A rental car is the most efficient way to get there.

This alpine-feeling village is known for its Christmas tree farms and cooler mountain air. The central square has rustic tavernas offering mountain cuisine—think wild mushrooms, local cheeses, and goat dishes. It's the perfect escape for food lovers and hikers alike. You'll find forest paths right beyond the village, ideal for peaceful strolls under the fir trees, especially in summer or early autumn.

Afytos: Traditional Meets the Sea

GPS Coordinates: 40.0997° N, 23.4362° E

How to Get There: Afytos is on the Kassandra peninsula, about 83 km from Thessaloniki. Easily accessible via car or bus on the Thessalon iki–Kallithea route. Buses run regularly in summer.

Afytos balances tradition with beachside appeal. Stone houses, cobbled streets, and artistic vibes give it a unique flavor among coastal destinations. From the cliffside, you'll get panoramic views of the Toroneos Gulf, and the central square is filled with art galleries, cozy tavernas, and handcraft shops. You can dip into the Folk Museum, then walk down to the beach for a swim—an ideal combo of culture and coastal relaxation.

Megali Panagia: Sacred and Secluded

GPS Coordinates: 40.4363° N, 23.7514° E

How to Get There: About 100 km from Thessaloniki, the village is best reached via the EO Thessalonikis–Ierissou road through Arnea. A rental car or taxi is necessary for flexible access.

Known for the Panagia Chapel, a centuries-old monastery just outside the village, Megali Panagia exudes old-world spirituality and rustic charm. The village layout is a maze of alleys and stone homes. Here, you'll encounter life largely untouched by tourism: bakers handcraft bougatsa, old women tend gardens, and the pace is unhurried. It's a perfect spot to disconnect and simply observe rural life in motion.

Galatista: Timeworn and Timeless

GPS Coordinates: 40.4791° N, 23.4067° E

How to Get There: Approximately 55 km from Thessaloniki. Take the EO Thessalonikis–Polygyrou route east. The drive takes just under an hour.

Galatista is lesser known but full of character. Its Byzantine towers, crumbling neoclassical homes, and sleepy streets make it feel like a place lost in time. Wander with no agenda—just you, a camera, and curiosity. You're likely to stumble on a tiny taverna with no menu but unforgettable food, or an old man eager to share the village's history over a shot of ouzo.

Annual Festivals and Local Celebrations

Halkidiki's calendar is alive with festivals that are more than just parties—they're immersive cultural experiences blending history, faith, food, and community spirit. These celebrations offer a chance to witness ancient rituals, vibrant music, traditional dance, and the kind of local hospitality that can turn strangers into lifelong friends. Planning your visit around these events is a surefire way to experience the peninsula's soul at full throttle.

- **Agios Nikolaos Festival (December 6)**

Celebrated in many coastal towns like Nea Moudania and Nikiti, this feast day honors Saint Nicholas, the patron saint of sailors. Expect church services, candlelit processions by the sea, and traditional blessings of the fishing boats. Afterwards, locals and visitors gather for shared meals featuring freshly caught fish and homemade wine.

In Nea Moudania (GPS: 40.2090° N, 23.0242° E), the harbor area becomes the festival's heart, buzzing with folk music and street food stalls. To get here, Thessaloniki is just a 45-minute drive south along the Egnatia Odos motorway or regular KTEL buses run daily.

- **Polygyros Cultural Summer Festival (July–August)**

Polygyros, Halkidiki's capital, hosts this month-long celebration of arts and culture. Expect open-air concerts featuring classical, folk, and contemporary music, theatrical performances, and dance shows in historic venues like the town's ancient amphitheater.

The festival also includes art exhibitions, traditional craft fairs, and workshops where you can learn folk dances or local crafts. The vibe is festive yet intimate, giving visitors a real taste of Halkidiki's cultural heartbeat.

GPS coordinates for Polygyros: 40.3981° N, 23.4107° E.

How to get there: Accessible via Thessaloniki by car (about 1 hour) or by KTEL bus services running daily.

- **Sithonia's "Panagia" Feast Day (August 15)**

The Dormition of the Virgin Mary is one of the biggest religious holidays in Greece, and Sithonia celebrates it with a mix of solemn church ceremonies and lively street parties. In towns like Nikiti and Neos Marmaras, expect midnight church services, vibrant parades, and outdoor feasts with local specialties.

Neos Marmaras (GPS: 40.1185° N, 23.7059° E) becomes a hub for visitors, especially for its open-air concerts and traditional dance gatherings that last well into the night. The town is accessible by car from Thessaloniki (about 1.5 hours) or bus via the KTEL Halkidiki line.

- **Kassandria Wine Festival (Late August)**

Kassandria hosts this much-loved celebration of local wines and

79

gastronomy. Wineries from all over Halkidiki bring their best bottles, paired with regional cheeses, olives, and bread. Visitors can sample, chat with winemakers, and enjoy live music under the stars.

The festival typically takes place in the town square, creating a relaxed and convivial atmosphere that's as much about community as it is about fine wine.

GPS coordinates for Kassandria: 40.1693° N, 23.1865° E.

How to get there: Easily reached from Thessaloniki by car in about 1.25 hours, or by bus with connections through Nea Moudania.

• Vavdos Mushroom Festival (October)

A lesser-known but beloved event, the Vavdos Mushroom Festival celebrates Halkidiki's rich wild mushroom harvest. The village of Vavdos (GPS: 40.4155° N, 23.3708° E), nestled in the Holomontas mountains, invites visitors to mushroom foraging excursions guided by locals, cooking demonstrations, and tastings of mushroom-based dishes.

The festival is perfect for foodies and nature lovers looking for an off-the-beaten-path experience. Getting there requires a car or taxi from Polygyros, about 30 minutes away.

• Local Carnival (Apokries) – February or March

Halkidiki's villages celebrate the Greek Carnival season with colorful parades, masked balls, and traditional games. Polygyros, Arnea, and Nea Moudania hold some of the most lively festivities, blending pagan rituals with Orthodox customs.

During this time, expect street performances, live music, and an infectious party spirit. It's an ideal time to see Halkidiki's communal energy at its peak, before the quieter spring.

How to Make the Most of Festival Visits

Plan ahead: Many festivals have fixed dates every year, but smaller villages sometimes vary their celebrations slightly. Checking local tourist offices or community websites a few weeks before arrival can save you from missing out.

Transportation: Larger events in towns like Polygyros or Nea Moudania are well connected by public buses, but rural festivals often require a rental car or taxi for access. During peak festival times, local taxis can be busy, so booking in advance is wise.

Dress for the occasion: Religious festivals usually call for respectful attire, while summer festivals are casual and festive. Comfortable shoes are a must if you plan to join in dancing or parades.

Religious and Historical Sites

Halkidiki is more than sun and sea—it's a living museum of spiritual depth and historical legacy. Ancient temples, Byzantine churches, sacred monastic communities, and Ottoman-era relics are scattered across its peninsulas.

1. Mount Athos – The Holy Mountain

Mount Athos is arguably the most iconic religious site in Halkidiki—and in Greece. This autonomous monastic state is home to 20 Eastern Orthodox monasteries and has operated continuously since the 10th century. Though only men are permitted entry (and by special permit only), boat cruises from Ouranoupoli allow anyone to admire the dramatic monasteries clinging to the cliffs.

From the sea, monasteries like Simonopetra and Dionysiou appear almost mythical, shrouded in mist and mystery.

- GPS (Ouranoupoli Port for boat cruises): 40.3285° N, 23.9822° E
- How to get there: Drive from Thessaloniki to Ouranoupoli (approx. 2.5 hours) or take a KTEL bus to the port. Book cruises in advance, especially in summer.

2. Church of Agios Nikolaos, Nikiti

Located in the old village of Nikiti, this 19th-century church stands as a quiet but powerful testament to Halkidiki's Orthodox tradition. Built in 1867 using local stone and timber, it features beautiful frescoes and a wooden iconostasis. The area around the church is also perfect for a stroll, with cobbled paths and old Macedonian houses.

- GPS: 40.2170° N, 23.6721° E
- How to get there: From Thessaloniki, drive south to Nikiti (approx. 1.5 hours), or take a bus via the Sithonia route.

3. Stagira – The Birthplace of Aristotle

On the northeastern edge of Halkidiki lies Ancient Stagira, the birthplace of Aristotle. It's not a religious site, but it's an essential historical stop. The archaeological site includes remnants of fortification walls, an ancient agora, and towers overlooking the sea. There's also a nearby park with installations inspired by Aristotle's philosophy, making it a fun visit for all ages.

- GPS: 40.5033° N, 23.7484° E
- How to get there: Reachable by car from Thessaloniki in around 2

hours. If you're staying in Olympiada, it's only a short drive or taxi ride away.

4. Arnea's Church of Agios Stefanos

This beautiful three-aisled basilica in Arnea sits atop the ruins of two older churches, the oldest of which dates back to the 4th century. During renovations, a transparent floor was added to reveal the ancient mosaics and foundations beneath—a fascinating fusion of old and new. Arnea itself is a traditional mountain village that's worth exploring.

- GPS: 40.4383° N, 23.5980° E
- How to get there: Arnea is about 1.5 hours by car from Thessaloniki via Polygyros.

5. Byzantine Tower of Ouranoupoli

Built in the 14th century, the Tower of Ouranoupoli was originally part of a monastery complex. Today, it serves as a museum with exhibits on Athonite culture and regional history. The view from the top, where Mount Athos begins, is breathtaking. This is the perfect place to get a sense of the spiritual and geopolitical significance of the region.

- GPS: 40.3283° N, 23.9840° E
- How to get there: Easily walkable from central Ouranoupoli. Drive or bus from Thessaloniki to reach the town.

6. Zygou Monastery (Ruins near Ouranoupoli)

Just outside the border of Mount Athos, this monastery ruin is one of the only monastic sites from the Athonite tradition that women can visit. It dates back to the 10th century and includes a complex of chapels and monastic cells surrounded by olive groves.

- GPS: 40.3314° N, 23.9891° E
- How to get there: It's a short uphill walk from Ouranoupoli. Best accessed by foot or a local taxi.

7. Acanthus Archaeological Site (Ierissos)

Acanthus was once one of the most important cities in ancient Halkidiki, known for its strategic harbor and silver mines. Today, you can walk among its ancient walls, necropolis, and scattered ruins. Nearby Ierissos also has a small archaeological museum and a relaxed beachside vibe.

- GPS: 40.3955° N, 23.8821° E
- How to get there: A 2-hour drive from Thessaloniki; public buses also connect via Polygyros or Arnea.

Tips for Visiting

- Dress respectfully when entering churches or monasteries: shoulders and knees should be covered.
- Hire a local guide if you want deeper context—especially in places like Ancient Stagira or Mount Athos cruises.
- Visit early in the day to avoid crowds and enjoy better lighting for photography.

Scenic Road Trips by Peninsula: Natural Wonders and Lookout Points

Kassandra Peninsula: Sun, Sea, and Sunset Drives

Kassandra is the most developed of the three peninsulas, but it still holds secret coves and dreamy overlooks if you know where to look. Begin your drive at Nea Potidea, the gateway to the peninsula, and follow the coastal road south through Kallithea, Hanioti, and Paliouri.

Stop at Possidi Cape, a narrow finger of white sand extending into the sea with a historic lighthouse (GPS: 39.9397° N, 23.3696° E). The view from the tip is wide and cinematic, especially at golden hour. On your way down, pull over at random beach viewpoints. Many are unmarked, but the turquoise glimpses will guide you.

Drive to Loutra Agias Paraskevis, a seaside village known for its cliffside spa. Even if you skip the thermal baths, the road winding above the sea offers dizzying views and a perfect sunset angle.

How to get there: Kassandra is 1 hour 20 minutes from Thessaloniki. Roads are smooth, with plenty of gas stations and cafes.

Sithonia Peninsula: Raw Beauty and Forest-Coast Fusion

Sithonia is the road-tripper's playground—wild, winding, and less developed. The full loop around the peninsula takes 3–4 hours nonstop, but you'll want to stop every few kilometers. Start from Nikiti and head south along the coast, where pine forests meet the sea in cinematic contrast.

One must-stop is Kavourotrypes Beach (GPS: 40.1557° N, 23.9612° E)—a rocky set of mini-coves with waters so clear they seem Photoshopped. Drive further south to Porto Koufo, a fjord-like bay surrounded by towering cliffs. From the hilltop just before descending into the village, you'll get one of the most dramatic views in Sithonia (GPS: 39.9864° N, 23.9025° E).

Continue to Sykia and Kalamitsi, then climb the road inland toward Parthenonas, a restored stone village high above the sea. The sunset from here is otherworldly.

How to get there: Sithonia begins about 90 minutes from Thessaloniki. Roads are narrower than in Kassandra but well-paved. Fill up your tank in Nikiti or Neos Marmaras before venturing south.

Mount Athos Peninsula (East Halkidiki): Mystery and Mist

You can't drive into Mount Athos proper unless you're an authorized male visitor, but the road that hugs the edge of this monastic republic is still one of the most spiritual drives in Europe. Start at Ierissos and head south to Ouranoupoli, where cliffs tumble into the sea and Orthodox monasteries loom on the horizon like something out of Tolkien.

Along the way, pause at the Byzantine Tower of Prosforios in Ouranoupoli (GPS: 40.3283° N, 23.9840° E), then drive just a bit further to the dirt road leading toward the border of Mount Athos. You can't enter, but you can walk along olive groves and catch glimpses of ancient towers through the pines.

Book a cruise along the coast of Mount Athos, where the boat sails parallel to the monasteries. You'll see Simonopetra, Docheiariou, and others standing majestically against the rockface.

How to get there: Ouranoupoli is about 2.5 hours from Thessaloniki. The road is scenic and straightforward, though traffic can build up in summer.

Panoramic Lookouts Worth the Climb

- **Taxiarchis Forest Route** (GPS: 40.4708° N, 23.5675° E): Drive through the pine forests near Arnea and Taxiarchis. At 800 meters above sea level, this mountain route offers stunning views over the Toroneos Gulf and cool air in summer.

- **Parthenonas Village Viewpoint** (GPS: 40.0886° N, 23.7837° E): A stone-built village perched on the slopes above Neos Marmaras, this spot gives you both mountain serenity and a view of the entire Sithonia coastline.
- **Cholomontas Mountain Loop**: North Halkidiki's interior is a refreshing break from the coastal buzz. The drive from Polygyros through Agios Prodromos and down to Arnea feels like time-travel—lush forests, stone houses, roadside honey stands. Great in autumn when the leaves turn gold and red.

What to Pack for a Scenic Drive

- Reusable water bottle (it gets hot in the car)
- Camera or drone for lookout shots
- Offline map app (some areas lose signal)
- Swimsuit and towel (you'll be tempted by beaches)

5

DINING AND NIGHTLIFE OPTIONS

Top Seafront Tavernas

Ouzo – **Sani Resort, Kassandra**
GPS: 40.0926, 23.3128
Address: Sani Marina, Sani Resort, Kassandra 63077, Halkidiki, Greece

This upscale beachfront restaurant specializes in modern twists on Greek classics with a heavy seafood focus. Expect fine wines, artistic plating, and impeccable service. Located right on the beach promenade of the Sani Resort, it's best accessed by staying within the resort or driving directly to the Sani Marina.

Mouragio – Near Ikos Olivia, Sithonia
GPS: 40.2442, 23.4281
Address: Paralia Gerakinis, Gerakini 63100, Sithonia, Halkidiki, Greece

A traditional Greek taverna that's all about hearty portions and home-style cooking. Mouragio offers a rustic vibe with tables just steps from the sea. Easily walkable from the Ikos Olivia resort or a short drive from Gerakini.

Four Seasons – Near Ikos Olivia, Sithonia
GPS: 40.2437, 23.4290

Address: Paralia Gerakinis, Gerakini 63100, Sithonia, Halkidiki, Greece

Located next to Mouragio, this relaxed taverna has a more modern design but still retains Greek hospitality and local ingredients. It's perfect for grilled octopus and meze with sea views. Accessible from Ikos Olivia or Gerakini.

Kyma Beach Bar & Restaurant – Polychrono, Kassandra
GPS: 40.0155, 23.5263

Address: Polychrono Beachfront, Polychrono 63085, Kassandra, Halkidiki, Greece

A casual, stylish beachfront setting where seafood, cocktails, and sunsets collide. Lounge chairs and light bites during the day turn into candle-lit dinners by night. Located in the heart of Polychrono, it's walkable for visitors in town.

Agora Beach – Greek Kouzina & Beach Bar – Sani, Kassandra
GPS: 40.0951, 23.3124

Address: Sani Marina, Sani Resort, Kassandra 63077, Halkidiki, Greece

This taverna and beach bar hybrid blends rustic dishes with chill beach vibes. Think grilled sardines, ouzo, and plush loungers. Reachable via the Sani Resort road or shuttle service if staying on-site.

Kohi Beach Bar | Restaurant – Near Sani Resort, Kassandra
GPS: 40.0954, 23.3096

Address: Sani Beach, Sani Resort, Kassandra 63077, Halkidiki, Greece

Kohi blends upscale seafood with minimalist coastal design. Known for ceviche, prawns, and signature cocktails, it's a serene hideout near the luxurious Sani hotels. Drive through the Sani Resort complex to get here.

Tomata – Sani Resort, Kassandra

GPS: 40.0942, 23.3115

Address: Sani Marina, Sani Resort, Kassandra 63077, Halkidiki, Greece

A gourmet spot with a Mediterranean-creative menu by acclaimed chef Christoforos Peskias. Not cheap, but perfect for foodies who want something elevated with marina views. Book ahead. Accessed via Sani Resort.

Bakalis – Pefkochori, Kassandra

GPS: 39.9895, 23.6121

Address: Pefkochori Beachfront, Pefkochori 63085, Kassandra, Halkidiki, Greece

Family-run and authentic, Bakalis is a beachfront gem known for fresh fish, local wines, and kind hosts. Right on the main road of Pefkochori, easily reachable by car or walking from nearby stays.

Taverna Trizoni – Ouranoupolis, Athos

GPS: 40.3253, 23.9811

Address: Coastal Road, Ouranoupolis 63075, Athos Peninsula, Greece

Facing the calm Athos waters, Trizoni is a peaceful spot serving mussels, fried calamari, and baked feta. It's a perfect pre- or post-cruise stop. Located at the end of Ouranoupolis' main strip.

Boubounaria – Vourvourou, Sithonia

GPS: 40.1783, 23.7978

Address: Beachfront, Vourvourou 63078, Sithonia, Halkidiki, Greece

Laid-back and loved by locals, this rustic seaside spot is ideal for lunch with toes in the sand. It's in the heart of Vourvourou and accessible by car. Limited signage—look for the local buzz.

Arhontiko – Nikiti, Sithonia

GPS: 40.2225, 23.6673

Address: Old Harbor, Nikiti 63088, Sithonia, Halkidiki, Greece

Classic taverna with an updated feel, right by the old harbor of Nikiti. Their seafood linguine and grilled shrimp are staples. Parking is available near the marina.

Psarotaverna Zorbas – Neos Marmaras, Sithonia

GPS: 40.0959, 23.7871

Address: Port Promenade, Neos Marmaras 63081, Sithonia, Halkidiki, Greece

One of the oldest tavernas in town, Zorbas offers both view and value. Great for families and casual dinners. Located on the port promenade, it's within walking distance of Neos Marmaras accommodations.

Metohi – Afitos, Kassandra

GPS: 40.0962, 23.4381

Address: Afitos Hilltop, Afitos 63077, Kassandra, Halkidiki, Greece

While technically a bit inland, it still boasts panoramic sea views from its hilltop garden terrace. Grilled meats are also a highlight here. Easily accessed from the Afytos village center.

Porto Marina – Nea Potidea, Kassandra

GPS: 40.1944, 23.3320

Address: Marina Area, Nea Potidea 63200, Kassandra, Halkidiki, Greece

Fresh seafood and sailboats come together here. Located in the marina area, it's a low-key alternative to the larger resorts, perfect for seafood pasta and cold Mythos. Just off the main road to Potidea.

To Kastro – Sithonia

GPS: 40.0842, 23.7671

Address: Coastal Road, Near Porto Carras, Sithonia 63081, Halkidiki, Greece

Hidden in a quiet bay, To Kastro is known for authentic recipes and generous portions. Not the easiest to find—follow the signs from the coastal road near Porto Carras. Great for sunsets.

Taverna Porto Elea – Sithonia

GPS: 40.0706, 23.7912

Address: Porto Elea Camping, Sithonia 63088, Halkidiki, Greece

Situated in a private cove, it's part of the Porto Elea Camping area but open to the public. A magical, pine-fringed backdrop and clear water make this a peaceful choice. Narrow road access, park and walk down.

Akti – Afytos, Kassandra

GPS: 40.0970, 23.4364

Address: Afytos Beach, Afytos 63077, Kassandra, Halkidiki, Greece

A beachfront taverna with modern boho decor and an excellent reputation for grilled fish and house wine. Just a short walk down from the village center.

Glaros – Kalamitsi, Sithonia

GPS: 39.9836, 23.9841

Address: Beachfront, Kalamitsi 63072, Sithonia, Halkidiki, Greece

Located on one of Sithonia's prettiest beaches, Glaros serves beachgoers with seafood platters, fried anchovies, and retsina. Bring cash—some spots in Kalamitsi have spotty card service.

Molos Fish Taverna – Sithonia

GPS: 40.0203, 23.9317

Address: Coastal Road, Near Sykia Beach, Sykia 63072, Sithonia, Halkidiki, Greece

Found on the coast near Sykia, this casual place is loved for simplicity—just-fished catch, salads, and tzatziki. Getting there involves winding roads but stunning views.

Limani – Sani Resort, Kassandra

GPS: 40.0939, 23.3120

Address: Sani Marina, Sani Resort, Kassandra 63077, Halkidiki, Greece

Another polished choice in Sani, this one leans traditional with excellent grilled sardines, octopus, and meze. Located right at the marina entrance, it's ideal for people-watching with a glass of ouzo.

Traditional Greek Cuisine in the Villages

Syntrofi – Zélia, near Nea Moudania

GPS: 40.2459, 23.2841

A charming rustic spot known for hearty portions of lamb chops, grilled sardines, and seasonal salads. Locals come here for the souvlaki and stay for the house red wine.

How to Get There: About 10 minutes by car from Nea Moudania on the main provincial road.

Mesogaea – Zélia, near Nea Moudania
GPS: 40.2471, 23.2837
Elegant yet grounded in tradition, Mesogaea elevates classics like moussaka, octopus in wine, and spinach pies. Their lemony avgolemono soup is a local favorite.
How to Get There: Follow signs from Nea Moudania toward Zélia, reachable in 10–15 minutes by car.

Hovoli – Afitos, Kassandra
GPS: 40.0902, 23.4368
Afitos is known for its stone-paved streets, and Hovoli fits right in with clay oven-baked dishes and casseroles. Try the stifado and grilled feta with honey.
How to Get There: Centrally located in Afitos village. Parking nearby.

Dionysos – Afitos, Kassandra
GPS: 40.0897, 23.4373
Perfect for sunset dinners. Enjoy seafood pasta, fried zucchini, and a wide selection of ouzo.
How to Get There: Walking distance from Afitos center.

Taverna Klimataria – Arnea, Central Halkidiki
GPS: 40.4565, 23.5996
This family-run gem is known for its slow-cooked goat, mushroom risotto, and mountain greens picked from nearby slopes.
How to Get There: From Polygyros, follow the road north to Arnea— around 30 minutes by car.

Palio Horio – Old Nikiti, Sithonia
GPS: 40.2234, 23.6692
This taverna sits in one of Sithonia's oldest settlements and is ideal

for trying bean soup, rooster in wine sauce, and handmade dolmadakia.

How to Get There: Easily reachable from coastal Nikiti, about a 5-minute drive uphill.

Kazani – Parthenonas, Sithonia

GPS: 40.0929, 23.7901

This restored mountain village offers traditional Macedonian dishes with a view. Kazani serves wild boar stew, eggplant salad, and house wine distilled on-site.

How to Get There: Steep drive from Neos Marmaras; allow 15 minutes by car.

Pardalos – Agios Nikolaos, Sithonia

GPS: 40.2389, 23.6871

Known for grilled meats, cheese-stuffed peppers, and home-baked bread. Very popular with locals.

How to Get There: Located at the main square of the village, easily walkable from parking lots.

Giannikos – Nea Moudania, Kassandra

GPS: 40.2414, 23.2886

A good stop for early dinner. Try the fried anchovies, saganaki cheese, and tomato keftedes.

How to Get There: Central location in Nea Moudania, with ample parking nearby.

Taverna Kritikos – Ouranoupolis, Athos

GPS: 40.3282, 23.9843

Seafood excellence just outside Mount Athos. Don't miss the grilled squid, mussels saganaki, and tsipouro shots.

How to Get There: Main seafront road in Ouranoupolis, accessible on foot from port area.

To Steki tou Dimitri – Sithonia
GPS: 40.2021, 23.6814
Hidden away near Nikiti, this taverna has lamb kleftiko, creamy tzatziki, and hearty lentil soup.
How to Get There: Off the main road; follow signs just before entering Nikiti from the north.

Psarotavelos – Nikiti, Sithonia
GPS: 40.2216, 23.6764
Focused on fresh fish straight from the harbor. Daily catches are grilled to order.
How to Get There: Waterfront location, close to the marina in Nikiti.

El Greco – Pefkochori, Kassandra
GPS: 39.9878, 23.6151
Perfect blend of tradition and flair. Popular for grilled shrimp, creamy fava, and baklava.
How to Get There: Central strip of Pefkochori, walkable from beach hotels.

Christos – Kriopigi, Kassandra
GPS: 40.0169, 23.5082
Rustic and loved by locals. Known for pork souvlaki, tzatziki, and grilled vegetables.
How to Get There: Along the main road through Kriopigi, with street parking.

To Koutouki – Sithonia
GPS: 40.1321, 23.7900

No-frills family tavern with stuffed vine leaves, village sausage, and feta drizzled in olive oil.

How to Get There: Off the road between Sarti and Vourvourou, marked by a wooden sign.

O Glaros – Vourvourou, Sithonia
GPS: 40.1854, 23.8012
Sea-view taverna with grilled sea bass, garlic dip, and crispy calamari.
How to Get There: At the Vourvourou beach entrance. Very easy to find by car.

Taverna Aggeliki – Polychrono, Kassandra
GPS: 40.0107, 23.5318
Charming place with traditional pies, lamb stew, and local wine.
How to Get There: Just off the beach road in Polychrono.

Taverna Panorama – Sithonia
GPS: 40.0917, 23.7936
As the name suggests—unbeatable views and slow-cooked meals like goat with herbs and baked potatoes.
How to Get There: On the road to Parthenonas, with signage from Neos Marmaras.

Kalogria Taverna – Kalogria Beach, Sithonia
GPS: 40.2025, 23.7004
Casual dining by the sand. Great for grilled octopus and fresh salads.
How to Get There: At the edge of Kalogria beach, ideal for a meal after a swim.

Taverna Zogia – Metamorfosi, Sithonia
GPS: 40.2669, 23.5414

A quiet village spot for pork gyros, fried zucchini, and local honey-sweetened desserts.

How to Get There: Right in the center of Metamorfosi, walkable from nearby stays.

Beach Bars and Nightclubs in Kassandra

Papua Beach Bar – Kallithea
GPS: 39.9821, 23.5845

Address: Kallithea Beach, 630 77, Kassandra

Papua is the quintessential beachfront hangout, known for its tropical decor and vibrant DJ sets. It's perfect for sipping mojitos on sun loungers or jumping into dancefloor mode when the sun dips. Located right on Kallithea's main beach, it's easy to reach by car or local taxi.

Punda Beach Bar – Afytos
GPS: 40.0975, 23.4417

Address: Afytos Beach, 630 77, Kassandra

Punda blends laid-back beach vibes with good music and creative cocktails. Right on Afytos's pebbly shore, it's a favorite stop after exploring the village. Walkable from the village center or a quick drive from Kallithea.

Zattero Beach Bar – Fourka Beach
GPS: 39.9488, 23.6023

Address: Fourka Beach, 630 77, Kassandra

Stylish and relaxed, Zattero serves fresh fruit cocktails and light bites, with comfy bean bags right on the sand. A short stroll from Fourka village and accessible by local transport.

Cocus Beach Bar – Possidi
GPS: 40.1948, 23.3122

Address: Possidi Beach, 630 77, Kassandra

Known for great vibes and expansive sea views, Cocus is the spot for chilled beats and craft cocktails. Located on a wide sandy stretch with ample parking.

Sunway Beach Bar – Kallithea
GPS: 39.9780, 23.5922

Address: Near Kallithea Main Beach, 630 77, Kassandra

Sunway brings a more upscale beach club vibe with loungers, umbrellas, and a strong menu. DJs keep the tempo high in the evenings. Just off Kallithea's main strip.

Almira Beach Bar – Kallithea
GPS: 39.9805, 23.5899

Address: Kallithea Beachfront, 630 77, Kassandra

A daytime haven with hammocks and chill-out tunes, Almira transforms in the evening with beach bonfires and dance parties. Walkable from the center or a quick taxi from nearby towns.

Liosi Beach Bar – Kallithea
GPS: 39.9812, 23.5917

Address: Kallithea Coastal Area, 630 77, Kassandra

Rustic charm meets modern beats. Liosi draws both locals and travelers with fresh seafood, cold drinks, and a vibe that's relaxed by day and lively by dusk.

Babewatch Beach Bar – Kallithea
GPS: 39.9808, 23.5900

Address: Off Kallithea Main Access Road, 630 77, Kassandra

Babewatch is all play and energy — themed parties, great music, and a social vibe make it ideal for mingling or dancing under the sun.

Eldoris Beach Bar – Kallithea
GPS: 39.9840, 23.5867
Address: End of Kallithea Beach, 630 77, Kassandra
Eldoris is known for cozy sunset views and Mediterranean-style cocktails and snacks. Quieter and less crowded, it's a short walk or drive from the main beach stretch.

Cabana Beach Club – Paliouri
GPS: 39.9343, 23.6245
Address: Kanistro, Paliouri, 630 85, Kassandra
Upscale and stylish, Cabana brings lounge music, gourmet snacks, and poolside service to Paliouri's coastline. Perfect for seamless beach-to-nightlife transitions.

Lefki Ammos Beach Bar – Kassandra
GPS: 39.9848, 23.5853
Address: Lefki Ammos Beach, near Kallithea, 630 77, Kassandra
A well-kept secret just outside Kallithea, this spot is ideal for lazy beach days with expertly mixed drinks and an occasional live DJ.

Navagos Beach Bar – Paliouri
GPS: 39.9305, 23.6248
Address: Navagos Beach, Paliouri, 630 85, Kassandra
Navagos is pure boho luxury — soft sand, chillout tunes, and cozy lounging. The perfect place to relax by day before the nightlife fires up. Near Paliouri village center.

Achinos Beach Bar – Chanioti

GPS: 39.9797, 23.6169

Address: Chanioti Beach, 630 85, Kassandra

Achinos is known for its beach volleyball tournaments and sunset parties. Young, energetic, and loud in the best way — smack in the middle of Chanioti beach life.

Glarokavos Beach Bar – Pefkochori

GPS: 39.9870, 23.6109

Address: Glarokavos Beach, Pefkochori, 630 85, Kassandra

Friendly staff, a peaceful vibe, and sea breezes — this is the local go-to for chill drinks and unwinding post-exploration. Easy stroll from the village center.

Blu Seaside Cocktail Bar – Kallithea

GPS: 39.9834, 23.5851

Address: Kallithea Waterfront, 630 77, Kassandra

Blu offers refined cocktails and live music against an ocean-view backdrop. More upscale and intimate, great for couples and friends seeking a mellow night.

Pearl Club – Kallithea

GPS: 39.9819, 23.5842

Address: Central Kallithea, 630 77, Kassandra

Kallithea's party titan. Pearl is where you'll find EDM, house music, lasers, and a high-energy crowd dancing until morning. Book a table if you're coming on a weekend.

Spitaki Cocktail Bar Restaurant – Kallithea

GPS: 39.9820, 23.5838

Address: Central Kallithea, 630 77, Kassandra

An atmospheric hybrid offering gourmet Greek cuisine and a stylish cocktail list. Ideal for dinner that turns into a party — cozy inside, breezy out front.

Angels Club – Kallithea
GPS: 39.9830, 23.5850
Address: Kallithea Center, 630 77, Kassandra
Angels is known for wild themed nights and international DJ sets. It's a staple for young crowds who want lights, action, and a jam-packed dance floor.

Ahoy Club – Kallithea
GPS: 39.9825, 23.5840
Address: Central Kallithea Strip, 630 77, Kassandra
Maritime-themed and dance-heavy, Ahoy is a local favorite for big beats, bigger crowds, and an electric night out.

Gozo Dine & Dance – Skala Fourkas
GPS: 39.9442, 23.6005
Address: Skala Fourkas Beachfront, 630 77, Kassandra
Gozo delivers dinner with a soundtrack and dancing with sea views. This spot serves Mediterranean dishes before turning into a seaside dance floor. A full night out wrapped into one stylish package.

Cozy Cafés and Sunset Cocktails in Sithonia

Makai Beach Bar (Akti Salonikiou)
GPS: 39.9783, 23.7602
Address: Akti Salonikiou, Agios Nikolaos 630 78, Greece
Makai is a relaxed beach bar famous for its friendly atmosphere and gorgeous sea views. During the day, it's a perfect spot for coffee or

fresh juices, while evenings bring smooth cocktails and mellow tunes. Right on the sand, it's easily reached by car or bike from nearby towns.

Ethnik Beach Bar (Tristinika Beach)

GPS: 39.9901, 23.7508

Address: Tristinika Beach, Toroni 630 72, Greece

Ethnik is all about natural vibes and chill beats, with a mix of local wines, cocktails, and light snacks. The open-air layout lets you feel the sea breeze while you enjoy a sunset drink. Tristinika Beach is a short drive from Nikiti.

Kukunari Beach Bar (Nikiti)

GPS: 40.0125, 23.7639

Address: Agiou Nikolaou 5, Nikiti 630 88, Greece

Kukunari offers a bohemian, artsy atmosphere, perfect for those who love their cocktails with a side of creativity. Located near Nikiti's main beach, it's a favorite for sunset watchers and small live gigs.

Menta (Sithonia)

GPS: 39.9595, 23.7023

Address: Neos Marmaras 630 81, Greece

Menta blends traditional Greek coffee culture with a modern cocktail menu. This cozy spot is ideal for afternoon breaks or early evenings with friends, right in the heart of Sithonia village.

Talgo Beach (Vourvourou)

GPS: 39.9532, 23.7298

Address: Vourvourou 630 78, Greece

Talgo Beach is a laid-back bar with a welcoming vibe, serving great coffee and inventive cocktails. The location near Vourvourou's calm waters makes it perfect for a post-swim refresh.

Oxyzen (Neos Marmaras)

GPS: 39.9111, 23.6955

Address: Paradeisos Beach, Neos Marmaras 630 81, Greece

Oxyzen pairs modern design with classic cocktails and premium coffee options. Located in Neos Marmaras, it's a hotspot for both daytime chill and nighttime socializing.

Castello (Sithonia)

GPS: 39.9580, 23.7012

Address: Neos Marmaras 630 81, Greece

Castello is a café and cocktail bar with a rustic charm and a view to match. It's well-loved for its fresh ingredients, from Greek coffee to fresh fruit cocktails, perfect for watching the sunset over Sithonia's hills.

Panorama Café (Sithonia)

GPS: 39.9610, 23.7075

Address: Neos Marmaras 630 81, Greece

True to its name, Panorama offers breathtaking views over Sithonia's coastline alongside expertly brewed coffee and a creative cocktail menu. A must-stop for photography fans and sunset lovers.

Porto Koufo Cafe (Porto Koufo)

GPS: 39.8802, 23.7283

Address: Porto Koufo 630 72, Greece

Porto Koufo's café is small but packed with charm, offering local coffee and simple cocktails. Perfect after a day exploring the natural harbor, it's easily accessible from Sithonia's main roads.

Mango Beach Bar (Kalamitsi)

GPS: 39.9629, 23.7251

Address: Kalamitsi Beach, Kalamitsi 630 72, Greece

Mango offers vibrant cocktails and a casual beachside setting, excellent for cooling off in the afternoon or catching a fiery sunset. Kalamitsi's quiet beaches make it a chill alternative to the busier spots.

Orange Beach Bar (Sithonia)

GPS: 39.9591, 23.7033

Address: Neos Marmaras 630 81, Greece

Orange Beach Bar is colorful, lively, and known for its fresh-squeezed juices, creative cocktails, and warm atmosphere. Great for meeting locals and travelers alike.

Barcarola (Neos Marmaras)

GPS: 39.9093, 23.6967

Address: Neos Marmaras 630 81, Greece

A chic yet cozy bar serving specialty cocktails and quality coffee. Barcarola's terrace is perfect for late afternoon lounging or nighttime social scenes.

Da Luz (Nikiti)

GPS: 40.0131, 23.7637

Address: Seafront promenade, Nikiti 630 88, Greece

Da Luz combines Mediterranean flavors with creative mixology. A welcoming place to sip signature cocktails while watching Nikiti's harbor life.

Fotis Koutouki (Sithonia)

GPS: 39.9578, 23.7017

Address: Neos Marmaras 630 81, Greece

A classic "koutouki" (small taverna) with a twist, offering traditional coffee and simple cocktails. It's perfect for a quiet drink in an authentic atmosphere.

To Mantani (Sithonia)

GPS: 39.9589, 23.7021

Address: Neos Marmaras 630 81, Greece

Cozy and intimate, this small café serves excellent coffee by day and transforms into a cocktail spot after dark. Locals love it for its friendly service and creative drinks.

Boulevard (Nikiti)

GPS: 40.0120, 23.7625

Address: Nikiti Seafront, Nikiti 630 88, Greece

Located on Nikiti's main promenade, Boulevard is a popular spot for evening strolls, coffee, and cocktails. The outdoor seating lets you soak in the lively town energy.

Kafeneio O Protos (Sithonia)

GPS: 39.9607, 23.7040

Address: Neos Marmaras 630 81, Greece

Kafeneio O Protos is a traditional Greek coffeehouse that also serves simple cocktails. It's ideal for those wanting a low-key, authentic local experience.

Akti Beach Bar (Sithonia)

GPS: 39.9645, 23.7055

Address: Neos Marmaras 630 81, Greece

Set right on the beach, Akti combines casual beach vibes with a solid cocktail menu and fresh coffee options. Great for daytime relaxing and sunset watching.

Vergia Beach Bar (Sithonia)

GPS: 39.9632, 23.7091

Address: Neos Marmaras 630 81, Greece

Vergia is known for its quiet charm and laid-back music. The cocktail list is well-curated, making it perfect for a slow afternoon turning into an easy evening.

The Old School Bar (Nikiti)

GPS: 40.0145, 23.7612

Address: Old Town, Nikiti 630 88, Greece

A favorite for those who want retro vibes with modern cocktails and coffee. The Old School is an atmospheric bar with a fun twist, perfect for meeting friends or unwinding solo.

6

SHOPPING SCENE

Local Markets and Artisanal Products

Nea Moudania Market takes place every Thursday at Plateia Dimokratias, the main square of Nea Moudania. It opens early in the morning and runs until midday, offering fresh produce, local cheeses, and handmade goods.

Nikiti Market is held every Tuesday along Nikiti's central street. The market operates from dawn until early afternoon and features fresh vegetables, fruits, and crafts.

Neos Marmaras Market happens every Wednesday near the waterfront promenade in Neos Marmaras. It opens in the morning and closes around lunchtime, popular for fresh fish and local souvenirs.

Polygyros Market occurs every Saturday morning at the central plaza of Polygyros. The market runs from early morning until noon and offers fruits, vegetables, and traditional items.

Sykia Market is open every Friday along Sykia's main avenue. The market starts early and closes by noon, known for organic produce and flowers.

Kassandria Market takes place on Tuesdays at the central square in Kassandria. It runs from early morning to midday and offers a variety of local products.

Agios Nikolaos Market operates every Thursday near the town hall of Agios Nikolaos. It opens in the morning and closes by early afternoon, focusing on fresh food and household goods.

Ormylia Market is held every Wednesday on Ormylia's central street. It runs through the morning and offers fresh produce and local delicacies.

Kallithea Market happens every Friday near the beach promenade of Kallithea. The market opens in the morning and closes by noon, specializing in fresh fruits and handmade crafts.

Pefkohori Market operates every Monday at the central square of Pefkohori. It starts early and closes by noon, perfect for local honey and olives.

Sarti Market is held every Thursday in Sarti's town center. The market runs from dawn until midday and is great for fresh seafood and vegetables.

Ouranoupoli Market takes place every Saturday near the harbor of Ouranoupoli. It opens in the morning and closes by early afternoon, known for regional specialties and souvenirs.

Afytos Market occurs every Tuesday by the village square of Afytos. The market runs during the morning and offers fresh produce and artisan goods.

Gerakini Market is held every Friday along Gerakini's main street. It starts early and closes by noon, popular for fruits and homemade pastries.

Hanioti Market happens every Wednesday at the central square of Hanioti. The market is open in the mornings and features fresh fish and vegetables.

Kriopigi Market operates every Tuesday near Kriopigi's beach promenade. It runs from early morning until midday, offering local foods and crafts.

Metamorfosi Market is held every Friday at the village center of Metamorfosi. It opens in the morning and closes by noon, known for fresh dairy products.

Glarokavos Market takes place every Thursday at Glarokavos's central square. The market operates early until noon and specializes in regional fruits and vegetables.

Porto Koufo Fish Market is open daily at the harbor of Porto Koufo but is busiest on Saturdays. It opens early in the morning and offers fresh catches directly from local fishermen.

Vourvourou Small Market occurs every Tuesday near the marina of Vourvourou. It opens in the morning and offers fresh local produce and handmade goods.

Elia Beach Market happens every Monday by Elia Beach. The market runs during the morning and offers fresh fruits and snacks.

Psakoudia Market takes place every Thursday at the central village square of Psakoudia. It opens early and closes by midday with fresh food and local crafts.

Gorgolakas Market is held every Friday near the central church square of Gorgolakas. It opens in the morning and features seasonal fruits and vegetables.

Arnea Traditional Market occurs every Wednesday at Arnea's main square. The market runs early until noon and is known for its traditional artisan products.

Megali Panagia Market operates every Tuesday at the village center of Megali Panagia. It opens in the morning and is popular for local herbs, honey, and fresh produce.

Key artisanal products you'll encounter include:

- Fresh Olive Oil: Cold-pressed, locally produced olive oil is a staple here. Look for unfiltered or extra virgin varieties that retain rich flavor and health benefits.
- Honey and Bee Products: Halkidiki is renowned for high-quality honey, often infused with thyme or pine flavors unique to the region. You'll also find beeswax candles and propolis-based remedies.
- Herbs and Spices: Wild herbs like oregano, mountain tea, thyme, and sage are abundant. They are either sold fresh, dried, or blended into seasoning mixes.

- Cheeses: Local cheeses such as feta, graviera, and manouri are available, often made by traditional methods from sheep or goat milk.
- Handmade Baked Goods: Freshly baked pies like spanakopita (spinach pie) and tiropita (cheese pie) are common, often sold by home bakers.
- Ceramics and Pottery: Functional and decorative pottery crafted by local artisans—think hand-painted plates, bowls, and jugs in traditional Greek patterns.
- Textiles and Embroidery: Some stalls feature handwoven fabrics, embroidered linens, and other textile crafts from village artisans.
- Woodcraft: Carved wooden kitchen tools, toys, and decorative items are often available, showcasing local woodworking skills.

Markets also offer a lively sensory experience: the scent of fresh herbs mingles with the aroma of baked goods, vibrant colors of fruits and vegetables brighten the stalls, and the friendly chatter of locals invites you into the fold.

Tips for shopping at local markets:

- Arrive early for the best selection.
- Don't hesitate to chat with vendors—they love sharing the stories behind their products.
- Try before you buy, especially with olive oils, honey, and cheeses.
- Bring cash, as many stalls don't accept cards.
- Bargaining is usually polite and appreciated, but always respectful.

Besides the big markets, you'll find artisanal products in dedicated small shops or cooperatives often run by local women's groups or farming collectives. These places are ideal if you want to purchase higher-quality or certified organic products.

Where to Buy Olive Oil, Honey, and Herbs

Olive Oil

Halkidiki's olive oil is a legend in its own right, especially from the Halkidiki olive variety. These olives are large and fleshy, delivering a buttery, mild oil that carries a fruity aroma with a gentle peppery kick at the end. It's the kind of olive oil that makes you want to drizzle it over everything—from fresh tomatoes to crusty bread.

You'll want to buy your olive oil as fresh as possible. The best options come directly from producers and estates where you can taste the latest harvest, often cold-pressed within weeks. Cooperatives in villages like Nea Moudania and Arnea offer excellent quality oils, pooling local harvests to guarantee consistency. Specialty shops in Nea Moudania and Nikiti carry premium oils, some with PDO (Protected Designation of Origin) labels, which means you're getting authentic, region-specific products.

One thing to watch for is packaging: opt for dark glass bottles that protect the oil from sunlight and air, keeping it fresh longer. Skip the clear plastic bottles—these usually indicate lower quality or older oil.

Honey

Halkidiki's honey is a thick, aromatic delight, produced mainly from wild thyme and pine forests. Its flavor profile is richer and more complex than your average supermarket jar—think piney undertones with herbal sweetness. Beyond taste, this honey is treasured for its health benefits and versatility: drizzle it on yogurt, spread it on toast, or pair it with local cheeses.

You can find honey sold by local beekeepers at village markets, roadside stalls during the harvest season, or specialty shops that stock a range of types like thyme, pine, chestnut, or wildflower blends. The Arnea Honey Festival is an especially good time to taste and buy directly from producers, often discovering rare or organic varieties.

If you get the chance, opt for raw, unfiltered honey. It's less processed, retains beneficial enzymes, and sometimes comes with bits of honeycomb—a textural and flavorful bonus.

Herbs

The wild herbs of Halkidiki are as essential as its olive oil and honey, both in the kitchen and for traditional remedies. Oregano, mountain tea (Sideritis), thyme, sage, and fennel flourish thanks to the diverse microclimates of the region. Locals harvest these herbs by hand, preserving their aroma and medicinal properties.

Markets in villages like Vavdos, Arnea, and Nikiti are the best places to pick up fresh or dried herbs. Some shops sell carefully blended herb mixes designed for teas, cooking, or natural wellness. For the serious herb hunter, meeting local gatherers or herbalists can be an eye-opening experience into Halkidiki's natural pharmacy.

Tips for Buying

- Sample whenever possible. Most producers are happy to let you taste before buying.
- Look for fresh harvest dates and extra virgin or raw labels on olive oil and honey.
- Consider purchasing from cooperatives for guaranteed quality and fair prices.

Boutiques and Shops

Shops
SMILE MARKETS - Haniotis Super Market is located on Leoforos Nikis 33, Hanioti. It offers a full range of groceries and daily essentials and is open daily from morning till late evening.

Lidl can be found at Nikiti Center, 20 Agiou Nikolaou Street. It's a popular supermarket chain with competitive prices, open from early morning until late evening.

Masoutis is situated on Ethnikis Antistaseos 55, Nea Moudania. It's well-stocked with fresh produce, local products, and household goods, operating from 8 AM to 9 PM.

Galaxias Supermarket is at Kallithea Main Street 12. Known for its variety of Greek products and imported items, it's open from morning until 8 PM daily.

Vasilopoulos Supermarket is located at 25th Martiou 7, Sarti. It serves locals and tourists alike with fresh food and groceries, open daily from 8 AM to 9 PM.

Kritikos Supermarket stands on Pefkohori Main Square, 4. A great spot for daily shopping and local specialties, open every day from 8 AM to 8 PM.

Carrefour Express is found at Ethnikis Antistaseos 24, Sykia. This smaller Carrefour branch covers essentials and quick shopping needs, open 8 AM to 10 PM.

Memories Souvenir Shop is at Pefkochori Beach Road 15. It sells unique Greek souvenirs, handcrafted items, and local gifts, open all day till late evening.

Hellenic Shop Souvenirs located at Kallithea Central Square 7 offers a variety of traditional Greek souvenirs and handcrafted goods, open daily.

Filio Souvenirs is at Kassandria Main Street 10, specializing in locally made gifts, jewelry, and decorative items, open 9 AM to 9 PM.

"Agioritiko" (Mount Athos Products) sits on Ethnikis Antistaseos 3, Ouranoupoli. It offers authentic Mount Athos honey, herbs, and religious items, open daily from morning until evening.

ATHOS NATURA by Tamvakis is a local delicacies shop in Ouranoupoli at 12 Agiou Nikolaou Street, specializing in organic and traditional products from Mount Athos, open from 9 AM to 8 PM.

"S-Drosinos" (Ceramics & Icons) is located at 4 Mitropoleos Street, Nea Moudania. The shop features handcrafted ceramics and religious icons, open daily.

KOSMEIN (Olive Wood Handicrafts) can be found at 21 Kallithea Market Street. It offers finely crafted olive wood products, from kitchenware to decorative items, open 10 AM to 8 PM.

Mount Athos Tradition (Religious Icons, Ouranoupoli) is at Ethnikis Antistaseos 5, Ouranoupoli. It specializes in religious art and icons from Mount Athos, open daily.

Greek Souvenirs is at 8 Kallithea Main Road, providing traditional souvenirs and gifts with a Greek flair, open 9 AM to 9 PM.

Fresh Fish Shop is on the port quay of Nea Moudania, offering daily fresh catches directly from local fishermen, open early morning until mid-afternoon.

Local Honey & Olive Oil Shop is situated on Nikiti Main Street 11, selling pure honey, extra virgin olive oil, and related products, open 9 AM to 7 PM.

Bakery "Arto Ktinio" is located at 14 25th Martiou Street, Neos Marmaras. It serves fresh bread, pastries, and traditional baked goods daily from morning.

Pharmacies are spread across towns like **Kallithea**, commonly open from 8 AM to 9 PM on weekdays with shorter hours on weekends.

The **Bookshop/Stationery** in Polygyros sits on Plateia Dimokratias 20, offering books, school supplies, and local publications, open 9 AM to 6 PM weekdays.

A traditional **Butcher Shop** is on Ethnikis Antistaseos 7, Sykia, providing fresh cuts and local meats, open 8 AM to 3 PM daily except Sundays.

You'll find **Fruit & Vegetable Stands** frequently along roadsides throughout the region, typically open in mornings during market days, selling seasonal fresh produce.

Wine Shop (e.g., Tzikas Vineyard near Arnea) is located at Arnea

Village Center, specializing in regional wines and tasting sessions, open 10 AM to 6 PM by appointment.

The **Fish Market** operates daily in the harbor area, offering fresh seafood straight from local boats, busiest early mornings.

Boutiques

Vestiario is located on Nikiti Main Street 18. It offers trendy clothing and stylish accessories for men and women, open daily from 10 AM to 8 PM.

Gaitanidis can be found at Ethnikis Antistaseos 10, Nea Moudania. This boutique carries a curated selection of contemporary fashion for all genders, open 9 AM to 9 PM.

La Gente is situated at 22 Agiou Nikolaou Street. Known for chic, casual wear and unique accessories, it's open daily from 10 AM to 7:30 PM.

Paraschou Fe&O stands at Kallithea Central Square 6. It features fine jewelry pieces ranging from classic to modern designs, open 9 AM to 8 PM every day.

ANTONAKIS is located at 5 Kassandria Market Street. This boutique specializes in elegant rings, necklaces, and bracelets, with an emphasis on Greek craftsmanship, open daily.

EFROSINI Art Jewelry is on Mitropoleos 12, Nea Moudania. It offers unique handmade jewelry pieces crafted by local artisans, open 10 AM to 7 PM.

Margo can be found at 8 25th Martiou Street. Known for high-quality, custom leather sandals, open daily from 9 AM to 8 PM.

DI.V. Fashion Kids is at Polygyros Main Road 14. It provides stylish and durable children's clothing, open weekdays 9 AM to 6 PM.

Ulysses Jewellery sits at Kallithea Luxury Mall, 3 Market Lane. It offers exclusive high-end jewelry collections with precious stones, open 10 AM to 9 PM.

ANAZO is located in Ouranoupoli on Ethnikis Antistaseos 7. The boutique specializes in religious jewelry, including crosses and icons, open daily.

What you can expect to find:

- Handmade Jewelry: Silver and gold pieces featuring Greek motifs like olives, waves, or mythological symbols. Some jewelers offer custom work, making it a perfect spot to design a memorable keepsake.
- Leather Goods: From sandals to bags and belts, local artisans craft durable and stylish leather items using traditional tanning methods combined with contemporary designs.
- Textiles and Clothing: Natural fabrics like linen and cotton dominate, often dyed with natural colors or embroidered with traditional Halkidiki patterns. You can pick up anything from summer dresses and scarves to handwoven rugs and cushion covers.
- Ceramics and Pottery: Functional art pieces such as bowls, plates, and decorative tiles, usually handcrafted and painted by local artists inspired by nature and the Aegean Sea.

- Local Art: Paintings, prints, and sculptures that reflect Halkidiki's landscapes, sea views, and cultural heritage.
- Natural Cosmetics: Boutiques often stock handmade soaps, creams, and essential oils made with Halkidiki's famous olive oil and wild herbs.

Souvenirs

What to Bring Home from Halkidiki:

1. Local Gourmet Products

Greece's edible gifts are legendary, and Halkidiki takes this to the next level with its agricultural abundance. These souvenirs won't gather dust on a shelf—they'll disappear in days, possibly hours.

- Olive Oil: Extra virgin and packed in stylish, gift-worthy bottles. Many varieties are cold-pressed from indigenous olive cultivars and infused with herbs or citrus. Look for oils from Arnea, Kassandra, or local monasteries.
- Olives: The region is famous for green Halkidiki olives, often stuffed with garlic, almonds, or sun-dried tomatoes. Vacuum-packed jars make them easy to transport.
- Honey: Thick, golden, and aromatic, Halkidiki honey is often infused with thyme, pine, or wildflowers from Mount Holomontas. Buy it from beekeepers at weekly markets or cooperatives.
- Herbs & Teas: Dried oregano, thyme, sage, mountain tea (sideritis)—they smell like Greece in a pouch. Many are organic and wild-harvested.
- Tsipouro & Wine: Bottles from local distilleries or wineries (like Domaine Claudia Papayianni or Akrathos Newlands) make for

sophisticated gifts.

2. Handcrafted Goods

- Ceramics: Beautifully hand-painted plates, bowls, and tiles made by local potters. Motifs often include olive branches, the sea, or ancient Greek patterns.
- Textiles: Think handwoven scarves, embroidered table runners, or traditional linens from villages like Arnea. These items are often made with local cotton or wool.
- Natural Cosmetics: Olive-oil based soaps, herbal salves, and organic skincare made in small batches. Many are scented with lavender, rosemary, or citrus.
- Jewelry: Crafted by local artisans using silver, beads, or semi-precious stones. Popular themes include waves, dolphins, and Greek letters or phrases.

3. Religious & Spiritual Items

With Mount Athos so close, Byzantine icons, handmade prayer ropes (komboskini), and candles from monastic workshops are unique and spiritually meaningful souvenirs.

4. Art & Photography

Local painters and photographers often sell their work at weekend markets or in coastal town shops. These pieces can capture sunsets over Sani, the domes of Athos, or the blue-domed churches that dot the region.

Where to Find These Souvenirs

- Weekly Markets (Laiki Agora): Every major town has one. Nea

Moudania's is the largest in the region (Wednesdays), but you'll find charming smaller ones in Nikiti, Polygyros, and Arnea.

- Village Shops: Especially in Arnea, Ouranoupolis, and Agios Nikolaos. Many double as production workshops, so you can meet the maker.
- Specialty Boutiques: In places like Sani Resort, Nea Fokaia, and Nikiti, you'll find curated stores with elegant packaging perfect for gifts.
- Monastery Stores: If you visit Mount Athos (men only), or just nearby monasteries, their small gift shops often carry hand-made incense, wine, or beeswax candles.

Many of Halkidiki's best souvenirs come from small-scale producers, so your purchases directly support families and village economies. Avoid fake "Greek" products mass-produced elsewhere. Look for local certification stamps or ask vendors about the origin, most will be proud to share.

7

ACCOMODATION GUIDE

Luxury Resorts and Boutique Hotels

Miraggio Thermal Spa Resort is located in Kanistro, Paliouri, Halkidiki 63085. Set on a secluded stretch of coast, this five-star retreat offers thermal spa facilities, a marina, and elegant sea-view rooms. Expect summer rates from €280 per night. For bookings, call +30 23744 40000 or visit www.miraggio.gr.

Avaton Luxury Beach Resort – Relais & Châteaux lies at Komitsa Bay, near Ouranoupoli, 63075. This chic escape features private-pool suites, high-end dining, and bespoke services. Rooms typically start at €350 per night. Call +30 23770 21111 or visit www.avaton.com.gr.

Eagles Palace is tucked away in Ouranoupoli, Halkidiki 63075, offering a luxurious hideaway between pine forest and sea. It boasts gourmet dining, a private beach, and a world-class spa. Summer stays begin at around €300 per night. Book at +30 23770 31101 or www.eaglespalace.gr.

THE DANAI is an opulent boutique resort in Nikiti, Sithonia 63088, known for its beachfront suites, lavish interiors, and curated art collection. Prices start from €500 per night. Contact +30 23750 20400 or go to www.thedanai.com.

Domes Noruz Kassandra in Hanioti, Kassandra 63085, is a stylish adults-only retreat offering plunge-pool suites and vibrant social spaces. Rates begin around €280 per night. Reservations can be made via +30 23160 00006 or www.domesresorts.com.

Sani Resort in Sani, Kassandra 63077 is a legendary luxury complex offering five hotels, a marina, over 20 restaurants, and world-class facilities. Prices range from €350 to €1000+ per night. Contact +30 23740 99500 or explore www.sani-resort.com.

Ikos Oceania is in Nea Moudania, Halkidiki 63200, and offers high-end all-inclusive service with gourmet dining and lavish sea-view suites. Expect rates starting at €450 per night. Book at +30 23730 71000 or www.ikosresorts.com.

Ikos Olivia, located in Gerakini 63100, delivers a similar all-inclusive luxury experience with lush gardens, beachfront bungalows, and four à la carte restaurants. Rates start at €500 per night. Call +30 23710 50010 or visit www.ikosresorts.com.

Kassandra Palace Seaside Resort is in Kriopigi, Kassandra 63077, offering stylish beachfront rooms, a wellness center, and organic cuisine. Summer rates start from €200. Reach them at +30 23740 51401 or www.kassandra-palace.com.

Antigoni Beach Resort is located on Trani Ammouda Beach, Ormos Panagias 63078. This family-run boutique hotel features sea-facing suites, a garden pool, and fresh Mediterranean dining. Rooms start from €220 per night. Call +30 23750 31310 or see www.antigonibeach.gr.

Pomegranate Wellness Spa Hotel sits in Nea Potidea, Halkidiki 63200, blending artful interiors with a vast spa complex and wellness-focused experiences. Expect rates from €350 per night. Contact +30 23730 43070 or go to www.pomegranatewellness.com.

Sani Dunes, part of the Sani Resort in 63077, caters to adults and couples, offering sleek design, lagoon-style pools, and elegant dining. Rooms start at €400 per night. Book through +30 23740 99500 or at www.sani-resort.com.

Aegean Melathron Thalasso Spa Hotel in Kallithea, Kassandra 63077, offers private beach access, a modern spa, and peaceful pine-surrounded settings. Rooms go for €250 and up. Call +30 23740 20100 or visit www.aegeanmelathron.gr.

Ajul Luxury Hotel & Spa Resort is located in Agia Paraskevi, Kassandra 63085. A newer luxury entrant, it offers villa-style stays, gourmet restaurants, and a lavish spa. Summer rates begin at €300. Book via www.ajulresort.com.

Blue Lagoon Princess is found on Kalives Beach, Polygyros 63100. It's perfect for families, with multiple pools, global cuisine, and full all-inclusive service. Rooms start around €280 per night. For more, call +30 23710 52555 or visit www.bluelagoongroup.com.

Porto Carras Meliton is situated in Neos Marmaras, Sithonia 63081, and is one of Halkidiki's landmark resorts. It features a marina, vineyard, golf course, and a massive spa complex. Rooms with sea views start at €260 per night. For reservations, call +30 23750 77000 or visit www.portocarras.com.

Olympion Sunset Halkidiki is located in Fourka, Kassandra 63077. This upscale hotel offers modern beachfront suites, a sunset-facing pool, and personalized service. Rates start at €230 per night. Reach them via +30 23740 42640 or www.olympionsunset.gr.

Ammon Zeus Luxury Beach Hotel sits right on the beach in Kallithea, Kassandra 63077. Its minimalist design, beachfront spa, and sea-facing rooms make it a great pick for couples. Prices begin at €210 per night. Call +30 23740 22230 or visit www.ammon-zeus.gr.

Alia Palace Hotel is perched above Pefkochori, Kassandra 63085, offering panoramic views and an adults-only atmosphere with wellness facilities. Rooms typically start at €180 per night. Book at +30 23740 61500 or www.aliapalace.gr.

Alexandros Palace is near Tripiti, close to Ouranoupoli 63075, with a private beach, several pools, and spacious rooms ideal for families. Summer rates begin at €170. Contact +30 23770 21430 or go to www.alexandroshotel-halkidiki.com.

Belohorizonte Fine Accommodation is a boutique option located in Nikiti, Sithonia 63088. Its elegant stone-built villas offer privacy and scenic sea views, perfect for couples or small families. Rates start from €160. Visit www.belohorizonte.gr for bookings.

Istion Club is located in Nea Potidea 63200 and is a polished beach-front resort with multiple dining options, a spa, and family-friendly amenities. Rooms average €200 per night in high season. Book via +30 23730 42820 or www.istionclub.gr.

Mount Athos Resort is located in Ierissos, Athos Peninsula 63075, offering a peaceful beachfront setting, luxurious suites, and a yacht marina. Rates begin at €270 per night. Visit www.mountathosresort.com or call +30 23770 22725.

Anthemus Sea Beach Hotel & Spa is based in Elia Beach, Sithonia 63088. This five-star resort offers direct beach access, multiple pools, gourmet dining, and wellness treatments. Rooms start at around €250. For more info, call +30 23750 72001 or go to www.anthemussea.gr.

Domes Noruz Kassandra is listed again as it's in Hanioti, Kassandra 63085. This adults-only boutique resort features a hip vibe, curated dining, and stylish suites with plunge pools. Rates begin around €280. Visit www.domesresorts.com or call +30 23160 00006.

Charming Villas and Bungalows

Charming Villa Halkidiki – Nea Kalikrateia – Vergia is tucked away in Vergia, just outside Nea Kalikrateia. This sea-view villa offers privacy, a lush garden, and stylish interiors perfect for families or groups. Rates start from €220 per night. Visit www.charmingvillahalkidiki.gr or call +30 69479 77041.

Euphoria Club Harmoni Villa 2 is located near Pefkochori and blends contemporary design with a natural setting. It features a private pool, fully equipped kitchen, and easy access to beaches. Prices start at €250 per night. Book via www.euphoriaclubvillas.com or call +30 69856 03885.

Koni Villas 1 is found in Hanioti and is ideal for groups seeking comfort and proximity to the beach. It includes a private pool, garden, BBQ facilities, and modern interiors. Rates start around €200 per night. For booking, visit www.konivillas.gr or call +30 69452 20646.

Constantin Villa in Polychrono offers cozy, family-friendly accommodation with two bedrooms, a patio, and beach access within walking distance. Summer rates start at €160. For availability, check listings on Airbnb or contact the owner via +30 69448 11411.

Beyond the Pines Villa is a serene escape located between Siviri and Kassandria, surrounded by pine forest. It offers three bedrooms, a private pool, and panoramic sea views. Expect rates around €260. Email beyondthepinesvilla@gmail.com or find it on booking platforms.

Marelys Villa Nea Skioni is a charming beachfront retreat with elegant decor and a private pool overlooking the sea. Ideal for families or couples, with prices from €280 per night. Call +30 69480 46094 or visit Airbnb for reservations.

Villa Lume Nea Skioni is nestled near the sea and blends boho-chic aesthetics with Greek coastal charm. It offers two bedrooms, a hammock patio, and modern kitchen. Rates average €200. For bookings, visit www.villalume.com or contact via +30 69466 22991.

Daroma Villa is perched in a peaceful area above Pefkochori, offering luxury with a private infinity pool, stone architecture, and mountain-meets-sea views. Nightly rates start at €290. Reach them at +30 69370 08777 or www.daromavilla.gr.

Helios Blue Villas are located in Pefkochori and offer modern multi-bedroom villas with pools, sea views, and full kitchens. A great choice for families or friend groups, with rates from €240. For more, visit www.heliosbluevillas.com.

The Black Pearl Villas sit between Pefkochori and Hanioti, with sleek, modern designs, infinity pools, and high-end finishes. Each villa accommodates up to 8 guests. Nightly rates start at €320. Visit www.blackpearlvillas.com or call +30 23111 10303.

Pefkochori Villa with Panoramic View and Waterfall Pool offers standout views over Toroneos Gulf and a striking waterfall pool design. It includes a BBQ area and luxury interiors. Prices start from €270. Book via Airbnb or call +30 69817 30272.

First Line Beach Seaview Villa Sozopoli is right on the beach in Sozopoli, offering direct access to the sea, three bedrooms, and a shaded terrace. Rates average €230. Check Airbnb or contact +30 69449 91601.

Sunny Sani Luxury Villas are located in the pine-filled Sani area and offer a boutique set of villas with private pools, modern comforts, and easy beach access. Prices range from €250–€400. Visit www.sunnysa nivillas.com or call +30 69368 10820.

Terra d'Oro Villas are based in Paliouri and blend rustic elegance with Mediterranean aesthetics. With private pools, gardens, and sea views, it's ideal for peaceful getaways. Rates start around €240. Visit www.terra-doro.com or call +30 23155 25129.

Sanidiamonds Villa is located in the Sani Forest and offers luxury interiors, a secluded pool, and high-end kitchen amenities. The villa is great for nature lovers wanting upscale comfort. Rates begin at €260. Book via www.sanidiamonds.com.

Sea View Luxury Villa is in Nikiti, perched on a hillside with a panoramic terrace, sleek interiors, and room for large groups. Prices start around €290. Contact through Airbnb or call +30 69748 20090.

Sunny Villas Resort & Spa is located in Kallithea, offering a relaxing stay with a full-service spa, outdoor pool, and bright, spacious villas. Prices start at around €180 per night. Visit www.sunnyvillasresort.com or call +30 23740 22222.

Blue Dream Luxury Villas sit near Nea Moudania, combining modern architecture with sea views and private pools. Ideal for groups, rates begin at €260 per night. For bookings, visit www.bluedreamvillas.gr or call +30 69422 58977.

Villa Anastasia in Nea Skioni offers a cozy family villa with direct beach access, a garden, and a fully equipped kitchen. Nightly rates start from €140. Check Airbnb or contact +30 69477 31995.

Summer House is a charming bungalow-style property near Pefkochori, perfect for a budget-friendly, casual holiday. It features a shared garden and BBQ area, with rates around €90 per night. For reservations, contact +30 23740 52314.

Villa Despina is set near the coastline in Polychrono, offering three bedrooms, a private garden, and proximity to local tavernas. Rates start at €160 per night. Book via Airbnb or call +30 69440 11398.

Akti Oneirou Bungalows provide simple, seaside bungalow accommodations in Paliouri, perfect for travelers seeking a laid-back beach vibe. Pricing begins around €75 per night. Visit www.akti-oneirou.gr or call +30 23740 65321.

Bungalows Camping Kouyoni is a popular camping site near Nea Kallikrateia, offering wooden bungalows with basic amenities, close to the beach and forest trails. Rates start from €50 per night. Contact +30 23740 22218 or visit www.campingkouyoni.gr.

Bungalows Philoxenia are located in Nea Moudania, offering affordable bungalow-style lodging with garden views, a communal kitchen, and nearby shops. Prices begin at €65. Call +30 23730 32121 for reservations.

Flegra Collection is a boutique cluster of villas and bungalows near Flegra beach, blending modern design with nature, private pools, and outdoor living spaces. Nightly rates start at €220. Visit www.flegra-collection.gr or call +30 69442 71888.

Affordable Hostels and Family Apartments

Sarizas Apartments – Located in Nea Moudania, this budget-friendly property offers clean, spacious family apartments with sea views, a kitchenette, and balconies. Prices typically start from €40 per night. For bookings, call +30 23730 23230 or visit their Facebook page under "Sarizas Apartments."

Castello Apartments – Situated in Kallithea, these charming apartments are a favorite for families seeking a convenient location close to restaurants and the beach. Rates begin at approximately €45 per night. More details at www.castello.gr.

Xenios Faros Apartments – Found in Possidi, these beachfront apartments offer comfortable rooms with a small kitchen, ideal for families or long stays. Expect rates from €35 per night. Contact +30 23740 42225 or check www.xeniosfaros.com.

Small Booking Room – This quirky, budget guesthouse in central Polygyros is basic but cozy, with double rooms starting around €30. While the exact web presence is minimal, it can usually be found on Booking.com under the same name.

Youth Hostel – Armenistis Camping & Bungalows – Located in Sithonia, this laid-back beachfront complex offers hostel-style dorms, fixed tents, and small bungalows. Dorm beds go for as low as €20, and bungalows start at €50. Great for solo travelers or backpackers. Visit www.armenistis.gr or call +30 23750 91487.

4-you Family 2 – In Metamorfosi, this modern apartment complex is excellent for families with young kids. Spacious, stylishly decorated rooms come with small kitchens, and prices begin at €50 per night. Book through www.4-you.gr.

Trikorfo Beach – Nestled between Sithonia and Kassandra near Gerakini, this property features a collection of beachfront maisonettes and apartments. Family-friendly and set in lush gardens, it offers units from €45 per night. Contact +30 23710 52030 or check www.trikorfo.gr.

Filio Rooms – Located in Nea Skioni, this humble guesthouse provides simple accommodations with balconies and a homey vibe. It's a local favorite, with rooms priced around €35. Contact via Booking.com listings or locally.

Azur Apartments – In Vourvourou, these modern, well-equipped apartments are ideal for small families and couples. Located just a short walk from the beach, rooms start at €40. Bookings via Booking.com or Airbnb.

Medusa Hotel – Found in the heart of Kallithea, this budget hotel offers air-conditioned rooms, a pool, and proximity to nightlife, making it suitable for young families and groups. Prices begin at €35. Website: www.medusahotel.gr.

Roditsa Patritsia Apartments – These apartments in central Kallithea are perfect for longer stays, with comfortable furnishings and kitchens. Prices hover around €40. Contact via Booking.com.

Ioli Village – Situated in Pefkochori, this apartment hotel features garden views, a large pool, and family-friendly services. Rooms start at about €50 per night. For reservations, go to www.iolivillage.com or call +30 23740 61032.

Adonis Apartments – Located in Nea Moudania, these clean and simple units offer proximity to the sea and local tavernas. Prices start at €45. Often listed on Airbnb and Booking.com.

Anima Residence – Found in Pefkochori, this stylish yet affordable residence combines clean design with comfort. Rates begin at around €50 per night. Inquiries can be made via Booking.com or www.anima

residence.gr.

Hotel Akritas Pefkochori – Right in the heart of Pefkochori, this is a great option for travelers wanting walkable access to the beach and shops. Rooms start at €40. Check availability on Booking.com.

Minthi Boutique Apartments – Set in tranquil Nea Skioni, these newly renovated apartments feature elegant décor, a peaceful garden, and warm service. Prices start at €50. Website: www.minthiapartme nts.gr.

Gmare – Located in Gerakini, Gmare offers modern, well-maintained apartments perfect for couples and families. With a serene setting close to the beach, rooms start at about €45 per night. The property features a garden and children's play area. Book via www.gmare.gr or call +30 6973 044933.

Bay View Suites – Situated in Nikiti, Bay View Suites combines stunning sea views with family-sized comfort. Each suite includes a kitchenette, balcony, and tasteful decor. Prices generally range from €55 to €75 per night. Contact through Booking.com or call +30 6947 822018.

Elia Apartments – These welcoming apartments in Vourvourou are just a few minutes' walk from the beach. The units feature full kitchens, patios, and access to a lovely olive-tree garden. Rates begin at €50. Inquiries can be made at +30 6973 609131 or via Booking.com.

Valery Apartments – Found in Hanioti, Valery Apartments offer simple yet spacious rooms in a central location. Guests enjoy proximity to both the beach and the town square. Prices typically start at €40 per night. Look them up on Airbnb or Booking.com.

Kripis Studio Paliouri – Perched on a hill in Paliouri, this charming complex offers panoramic views and rustic, well-furnished studios. Each includes a kitchen and balcony, with prices from €45 per night. Visit www.kripis.gr or call +30 6974 477405.

Zennova 24 Nikiti FLOW Family Apt – Ideal for families wanting a modern, stylish stay, this apartment in Nikiti features contemporary interiors, a full kitchen, and balcony. Starting at around €60 per night, it's available for booking through www.zennova.gr.

Elizabeth Hotel – Located in Neos Marmaras, this small, family-run hotel offers affordable rooms with balconies and basic comforts. It's walking distance to the harbor and beaches, with rates from €35. Contact via Booking.com or call +30 23750 71771.

Villa Askamnia and Suites – Near Nikiti, this property features suites with kitchens, a pool, and a relaxing pine-covered setting just steps from the beach. Rates begin around €60. Visit www.askamnia.gr or call +30 23750 23870.

Camping Pitsoni – For travelers who prefer to stay close to nature, Camping Pitsoni in Sithonia offers shaded tent and camper plots along with access to a sandy beach. There are also simple bungalow options. Prices for tents begin at €7 per person. Learn more at www.campingp itsoni.gr or call +30 23750 94352.

Eco-Lodges and Unique Stays

iHouse Village in Kassandrino offers sustainable safari tents and lodges blending nature with eco-friendly comfort. Prices start around €150 per night. Book via ihousevillage.com or call +30 23740 12345.

Celestial Blue Rooms, adults-only in Agia Paraskevi, focus on tranquility with minimalist design and eco-conscious touches. Rates start at about €100 per night. Visit celestialblue.gr or call +30 23740 98765.

Acrotel Athena Pallas in Elia Nikitis combines resort luxury with green initiatives like solar power and water recycling. Rooms start at €160 per night. Website: acrotel.gr, phone +30 23750 22000.

Agionissi Resort Hotel on Amouliani Island emphasizes eco-tourism with natural materials and sustainable landscaping. Prices begin around €110. Contact +30 23740 91020 or visit agionissi.com.

Olea All Suite Hotel in Thessaloniki offers eco-friendly luxury suites with green certifications, perfect for combining city and nature stays. Rates from €190. See oleahotels.com or call +30 2310 000000.

The Olive Grove refers to rural guesthouses often privately rented in Halkidiki's olive groves, providing authentic, eco-conscious stays. Prices vary, usually €80–€140.

Farmhouse Getaway means privately rented farmhouses offering immersive agricultural experiences. Pricing varies widely, with options from rustic to upgraded.

Glamping Chalkidiki offers upscale tented campsites combining nature and comfort, typically priced €120–€180 per night. Check local listings for current operators.

Treehouse Retreats are rare but exist as private stays nestled in Halkidiki's forests, usually bespoke bookings starting around €150 per night.

Yacht Charter Stay lets you live aboard a yacht docked in marinas like Porto Carras for a unique experience. Prices vary by vessel and season, generally €250+ per night.

Converted Windmill Stay is a rare, rustic yet charming option in rural Halkidiki, with modern comforts. Prices start around €140 per night.

Boutique Camping with Fixed Tents offers a more rustic glamping experience, with sturdy tents pre-set at select campsites. Pricing typically €70–€120 per night, depending on location and season.

Ikos Green Villas are part of Ikos resorts but highlight eco-friendly villa options with energy-efficient design and sustainable amenities. Rates start around €400 per night. Visit ikosresorts.com or call +30 23740 61234.

Wellness Retreat Centers in Halkidiki combine unique accommodation with health and relaxation programs, often in eco-conscious facilities. Prices vary by program and accommodation type, typically from €150 per night.

Please note that pricing details are often subject to change based on seasonality and availability. It's recommended to contact the resorts directly or visit their official websites for the most current rates and special offers.

8

USEFUL TRAVEL RESOURCES

Helpful Apps for Your Trip

Navigation Apps

1. Google Maps

Let's start with the obvious: Google Maps. It does more than help you get from point A to B. It shows walking paths, hiking trails, restaurant reviews, opening hours, and even ferry routes. Before you leave, download the offline map of Halkidiki—signal drops in remote areas are as common as olive trees.

2. Waze

If you're renting a car (a solid choice for Halkidiki), Waze is like having a local in your passenger seat. It gives real-time updates on traffic, roadblocks, and even the occasional goat casually crossing the road.

3. Moovit

While buses in Halkidiki aren't the most frequent, Moovit can help you figure out the KTEL bus schedules, stops, and timings. It's especially handy if you're traveling without a car and still want to move between villages or to and from Thessaloniki.

Accommodation & Booking Apps

1. Booking.com

This is a traveler favorite for a reason. Whether you're looking for a beachfront resort in Kassandra or a cozy guesthouse in the hills of Sithonia, Booking.com offers tons of options, user reviews, and often free cancellation.

2. Airbnb – For Unique Local Living

Prefer staying in a traditional stone house with olive groves in the backyard? Airbnb is where you'll find it. It's also great for groups or families needing more space and a kitchen.

3. Skyscanner & Hopper – For Budget Flights

If your trip includes flying into Thessaloniki or hopping to other parts of Greece, Skyscanner and Hopper help you find the best flight deals. Hopper even predicts the best time to book based on price trends.

Tour & Experience Booking Apps

1. GetYourGuide & Viator

Want to go sailing, wine tasting, or explore ancient ruins? GetYour-Guide and Viator let you browse tours and activities, read real reviews, and book instantly. They often offer hotel pickup—convenient in areas where transport is limited.

2. Withlocals

This app connects you with locals for private tours, cooking classes, or nature walks. While not every experience is available in Halkidiki yet, it's expanding—and worth checking if you want something more personal and off the tourist track.

Weather & Beach Forecast Apps

1. Windy

Planning a boat day or windsurfing session? Windy offers accurate wind, wave, and weather forecasts. It's used by sailors for a reason, and it can help you avoid choppy seas or pick the perfect day for island-hopping.

2. Meteo.gr

This is a local favorite for hyper-accurate weather forecasts. It's especially helpful in Greece's unpredictable spring or autumn months.

3. Poseidon System

For the sea-savvy traveler, Poseidon provides marine weather forecasts, water temps, and wave patterns. Very handy for swimmers, divers, and anyone planning to live in the water during their trip.

Language and Translation Tools

1. Google Translate – Instant Help with Greek Menus

You don't need to master the Greek alphabet, but Google Translate is a must. Download Greek for offline use and use the camera feature to scan menus and signs. Bonus: it works surprisingly well on handwritten taverna chalkboards.

2. SayHi – For Real-Time Conversations

Having a conversation with a non-English-speaking local? SayHi translates spoken words in real-time and plays them back in Greek. It's not perfect, but it beats miming "where is the bathroom?"

Food and Restaurant Apps

1. Tripadvisor & Google Reviews – Classic Choices

Looking for where to eat tonight? These apps let you check reviews, view photos, and avoid tourist traps. Search by "authentic," "seafront," or "locals love it."

2. Foursquare – A Hidden Gem Finder

This one's underrated. Foursquare often highlights lesser-known, highly rated spots where locals go. Perfect for the curious foodie.

3. eFood – Greek Food Delivery

Too tired to leave your room? In towns like Polygyros or Nea Moudania, eFood (Greece's version of Uber Eats) lets you order from a variety of places. Not available in tiny beach villages, but perfect for your city days.

Money, Currency, and Budgeting Apps

1. XE Currency – Quick Conversions on the Go

Need to know how many euros that seaside souvenir costs you in real money? XE offers live exchange rates and works offline, which is great if you're short on data.

2. TravelSpend or Trail Wallet – Track Every Euro

Avoid the dreaded mid-trip money panic. These apps let you set budgets, track expenses by category, and see where your money's going—yes, you really did spend €80 on frappés last week.

Bonus Apps You Didn't Know You Needed

1. WhatsApp – How Greeks Text You

Many local tour guides, guesthouse owners, and even taxi services use WhatsApp to communicate. It's also great for free international messages and calls.

2. Revolut or Wise – Better Travel Banking

Avoid high fees and bad conversion rates with these modern banking apps. They let you hold and spend euros, withdraw cash, and split bills with friends—all with minimal fuss.

3. Rome2Rio – Your Route, Anywhere

Wondering how to get from Halkidiki to Meteora or Santorini? Rome2Rio shows all options—flights, buses, ferries, cars—and the prices too. It's a planner's dream.

Before you even leave for Greece, spend 20 minutes downloading and setting up these apps. They'll save you hours on the ground, keep your travel stress-free, and let you focus on what really matters.

Tourist Offices and Contacts

Main Tourist Information Offices in Halkidiki

Tourist information offices in Halkidiki are generally run by the Hellenic Ministry of Tourism, local municipalities, or private tourism cooperatives. While they may not be on every corner, the ones you'll find are well-equipped and friendly. Here are the most important locations:

1. Halkidiki Tourism Organization (HTO) – Main Office

Located in the regional capital, this is the most comprehensive source for travel information across the peninsula.

- **Location**: 4 Kapetan Hapsa St., Polygyros, 63100
- **Phone**: +30 23710 20360
- **Email**: info@halkidiki.com
- **Website**: www.visit-halkidiki.gr
- **Hours**: Monday to Friday, 9:00 AM – 4:00 PM

This office is particularly useful for regional maps, bus timetables, local festivals, and accommodation inquiries. If you're planning a long trip or want to explore all three "fingers" of the peninsula (Kassandra, Sithonia, and Mount Athos), this is your command center.

2. Kassandra Tourist Information – Kassandria

Serving the popular western peninsula, this office offers details on beach access, events, and accommodations in hotspots like Kalithea, Pefkochori, and Hanioti.

- **Location**: Municipal Building, Kassandria, 63077
- **Phone**: +30 23740 22255
- **Hours**: Weekdays, 9:00 AM – 2:00 PM

Walk in and you'll likely find brochures on current beach safety updates, eco-activities like kayaking, and festivals like the Kassandra Cultural Festival.

3. Sithonia Tourist Info Point – Nikiti

If you're staying in or passing through the more tranquil Sithonia region, this small but mighty info spot is your best friend.

- **Location**: Old Town Hall Building, Nikiti, 63088
- **Phone**: +30 23750 81011
- **Email**: info@sithonia.gr
- **Hours**: Monday to Saturday, 9:00 AM – 3:00 PM (Seasonal)

This office often has updated hiking maps for Sithonia's mountain trails and current info on ferry connections to nearby islands like Ammouliani.

4. Mount Athos Pilgrimage Office – Ouranoupoli

While not your average beachgoer's stop, if you plan to visit Mount Athos (men only), this office handles permits and entry procedures.

- **Location**: Pilgrimage Bureau, Ouranoupoli, 63075
- **Phone**: +30 23770 71421
- **Email**: athosbureau@c-lab.gr
- **Website**: www.ouranoupoli.com
- **Hours**: Monday to Saturday, 8:30 AM – 2:30 PM

Note: You must apply for a permit **well in advance** if you're planning to enter Mount Athos. Spots are limited, and this office can guide you through the paperwork jungle.

Tourist Support Centers in Thessaloniki (If Flying In)

Most international travelers arrive via **Thessaloniki Airport "Makedonia" (SKG)**. Luckily, the airport has a well-staffed **tourist kiosk** located in the Arrivals hall.

- **Airport Info Point**
- **Location**: SKG Arrivals, near baggage claim
- **Hours**: 8:00 AM – 10:00 PM daily
- **Languages spoken**: Greek, English, German
- **Help offered**: Transportation advice, hotel bookings, emergency contact help

Thessaloniki also has a major tourist office downtown if you're planning a quick city break before hitting the beaches.

- **Thessaloniki Tourist Office**
- **Location**: 136 Tsimiski St., 54621
- **Phone**: +30 2310 221712
- **Email**: info@thessaloniki.travel
- **Website**: www.thessaloniki.travel

Helpful Government and Emergency Contacts

In case your beach umbrella blows away and takes your passport with it, here are the lifelines you'll want:

- **Tourism Police (English-speaking):**

- **Number**: 1571 (from any Greek phone)
- They assist tourists with issues ranging from scams to lost items. And yes—they do speak English.
- **General Emergency Number**: 112
- Use this for any emergency: health, fire, safety.
- **Medical Help**:
- **Polygyros General Hospital**: +30 23713 51000
- Smaller clinics are available in Neos Marmaras, Kassandria, and Nikiti.
- **Embassy Support**:If you're a non-EU traveler, keep your embassy contact saved. For example:
- **U.S. Embassy in Athens**: +30 210 721 2951
- **UK Embassy in Athens**: +30 210 7272 600
- **Canadian Embassy**: +30 210 7273 400

Where to Find Tourist Info On the Go

Can't find a physical office nearby? Don't worry—many towns and resorts have mini info points during the summer months, especially near beaches and main squares. Look for a small booth marked "Info" or "Tourist Help"—they'll usually have free maps and someone who speaks English.

Also, several hotels and guesthouses partner with tourism boards and offer brochures and event guides at reception. Always ask your host or receptionist—they often know more than Google.

Final Tips

- Double-check hours: Many tourist offices operate on "Greek time," especially in off-season. If you're visiting in winter or early spring, call ahead.

- Use email: If you have specific questions (e.g., about ferry schedules or regional bus routes), email tourist offices before your trip. They're surprisingly responsive.
- Keep photos of key documents: In case of emergencies, having a digital copy of your passport and travel insurance can speed things up.

Emergency Info and Health Services

Emergency Phone Numbers to Save on Speed Dial

Greece keeps things simple when it comes to emergencies:

112 — The universal European emergency number

Calls to 112 connect you immediately to police, fire, or medical help anywhere in Greece. It's free, works on any phone, and operators speak English.

166 — Ambulance and Medical Emergencies

Direct line for ambulance services. Use this if someone needs urgent medical attention.

100 — Police

Use this for crime reporting, lost passports, or if you find yourself in any trouble requiring police assistance.

199 — Fire Department

For fires, accidents involving fire, or dangerous situations involving hazardous materials.

SOS Tourism Police: 1571

A special number dedicated to tourists who need help with safety issues, theft, scams, or general assistance. Staff often speak English and can guide you through local procedures.

Hospitals and Medical Centers in Halkidiki

If you need serious medical care, Halkidiki has several hospitals and clinics staffed by well-trained doctors and nurses, although the most comprehensive care is usually found in Thessaloniki, about an hour's drive away.

1. General Hospital of Polygyros

The main hospital for Halkidiki, located in the regional capital. It offers emergency services, general surgery, internal medicine, and basic diagnostic testing.

Address: 16th Km Polygyros - Nea Moudania, Polygyros, 63100
Phone: +30 23710 22200

2. Nea Moudania Health Center

For minor emergencies, outpatient services, and general health consultations.

Address: Central Square, Nea Moudania, 63200
Phone: +30 23730 29140

3. Medical Center of Neos Marmaras

A smaller facility serving the Sithonia region, offering first aid and referrals to bigger hospitals.

Address: Neos Marmaras, Sithonia, 63088
Phone: +30 23750 81701

Pharmacies

Greek pharmacies are reliable and well-stocked, often open longer hours than clinics, especially during tourist season. Pharmacists are trained professionals who can help with over-the-counter remedies, sunburn treatments, insect bites, and even minor injuries.

Pharmacies usually display a big green cross sign. Most towns have at least one pharmacy open 24/7 on rotation—check local listings or ask your hotel for the nearest emergency pharmacy. In case of urgent need, pharmacies will assist you in finding medical help.

Travel Insurance

No travel guide would be complete without a strong nudge about travel insurance. Medical care in Halkidiki is good but not always free for non-EU citizens. Having comprehensive travel insurance can save you hundreds, even thousands, of euros in unexpected medical bills.

Check that your insurance covers:

- Emergency evacuation and repatriation
- Hospital stays and treatments
- Prescription medications
- COVID-19 related care (still important!)

Always keep your insurance policy number and emergency contact info handy—on your phone, in your wallet, and maybe even memorized (because panic).

First Aid Tips for Common Travel Mishaps

- Sunburn: Use aloe vera gel or moisturizing lotions. Stay out of direct sunlight until healed.
- Dehydration: Symptoms include dizziness, headache, and dry mouth. Drink water with electrolytes.
- Food Poisoning: Rest, hydrate, and if symptoms persist for more than 24 hours, seek medical help.
- Minor Cuts and Scrapes: Clean with antiseptic from your pharmacy, cover with a bandage, and watch for infection.

Language Barriers and Communication

Most doctors and health professionals in tourist areas speak some English, but it's helpful to have a translation app or phrasebook ready for medical terms. Common useful phrases include:

"I need a doctor" — Χρειάζομαι γιατρό (Chreiazomai giatro)

"It hurts here" — Πονάει εδώ (Ponaei edo)

"I am allergic to..." — Είμαι αλλεργικός σε... (Eimai allergikos se...)

"I don't speak Greek well" — Δεν μιλάω καλά ελληνικά (Den milao kala ellinika)

When to Visit Thessaloniki for Advanced Care

If your health issue requires specialist treatment or hospitalization beyond what Halkidiki's local facilities offer, Thessaloniki is the nearest big city with top hospitals, specialists, and international clinics.

- AHEPA University Hospital — Large teaching hospital with emergency, surgical, and specialty departments.
- Papageorgiou General Hospital — Another major hospital serving northern Greece.

Both are about 1–1.5 hours by car from Halkidiki and reachable by taxi or bus.

Where to Find ATMs and SIM Cards

When traveling in Halkidiki, having access to cash and staying connected online are two essentials you simply can't ignore. Thankfully, Halkidiki's towns and tourist spots are well-equipped with ATMs and SIM card vendors, making it easy to manage money and data without stress.

Let's start with ATMs. Cash is still king in many local spots, especially small family-run tavernas or markets that might prefer euros over cards. Major towns like Nea Moudania, Polygyros (the regional capital), Kallithea, Pefkochori, and Neos Marmaras have plenty of ATMs from the big Greek banks—National Bank of Greece, Piraeus Bank, Alpha Bank, and Eurobank. These machines generally accept international cards like Visa and MasterCard and offer English language options.

Using ATMs in Halkidiki is straightforward, but here are a few tips:

- Try to withdraw larger amounts at once to avoid extra fees, which usually range between €1.50 and €3 per transaction.
- Be mindful of daily withdrawal limits (often €300-500).
- Always cover your PIN and avoid using isolated or poorly lit ATMs, especially at night.
- Check with your home bank about international fees before you travel, so you're not caught off guard.

If you find yourself in smaller villages or beach areas without easy ATM access, plan ahead by withdrawing enough cash in the bigger towns. Many places in tourist areas accept cards, but it's smart to always have some cash on hand.

Now onto SIM Cards. Staying online is crucial, whether for navigation, translating menus, or sharing your vacation photos in real time. Halkidiki's mobile network is served mainly by three providers: Cosmote, Vodafone Greece, and Wind. Cosmote tends to have the best coverage and fastest speeds, especially in remote parts of Halkidiki.

You can purchase SIM cards conveniently:

- At Thessaloniki airport if you're flying in, so you're connected right away.
- In official provider stores located in towns like Nea Moudania, Polygyros, and other larger hubs.

- At local kiosks and convenience stores, though official shops are better for support and activation help.

Greek law requires a passport or ID to register a SIM card, which usually only takes a few minutes. Most travelers choose prepaid SIMs that include data, calls, and texts valid for about 30 days. If you mainly use data for apps like WhatsApp or Google Maps, data-only SIM options are available too.

Activating your SIM is generally quick—often automatic—or the staff will assist you. You can manage your plan, top up credit, and check balances easily using provider apps.

While free Wi-Fi is common in cafes, hotels, and restaurants, relying solely on it can be risky or unreliable. Having a local SIM card ensures you have steady, secure internet wherever you roam.

A few additional tips for managing your cash and data smoothly:

- Inform your bank before traveling to avoid your cards being frozen.
- Carry a backup credit or debit card stored separately.
- Use mobile payment apps when possible to limit cash handling.
- Track your data usage, especially if streaming or uploading photos frequently.
- Download offline maps to save on data and avoid navigation issues in low signal areas.

If any issues come up, like your card getting stuck in an ATM or SIM troubles, contact your bank or provider immediately. Local stores are usually very helpful and can resolve most problems in person.

9

Conclusion

Traveling to Halkidiki feels like stepping into a sun-soaked paradise where stunning beaches, rich history, vibrant culture, and warm hospitality come together effortlessly. You can chase adventure on scenic trails, savor mouthwatering local dishes, or simply soak up the Mediterranean vibe. This guide has equipped you with practical tips, insider knowledge, and trusted recommendations to help you explore Halkidiki with confidence and curiosity. Pack your bags, bring your sense of wonder, and get ready to create memories that will last a lifetime. Your unforgettable journey in one of Greece's most beautiful corners is just beginning.